MARITIME COOPERATION IN SOUTH ASIA

The Regional Centre for Strategic Studies (RCSS) is a South Asian regional think tank, based in Colombo, Sri Lanka. Established in 1993, it is an independent, non-profit and non-governmental organization which encourages research, dialogue, and deliberation on a broad range of conventional and non-conventional sources of conflict. The RCSS enables scholars and other professionals to address, individually and collectively, problems and issues of topical interest for all South Asian countries.

The Centre's key objectives are to:

- Sponsor, coordinate, and support research on South Asian strategic, security, and environmental issues.
- Promote interaction among scholars and professionals in the region and beyond who are engaged in South Asian studies.
- Foster linkages and collaboration among institutions focusing on studies and activities related to conflict, conflict transformation, and regional cooperation in South Asia.
- Encourage a new generation of analysts and commentators to generate fresh ideas and perspectives on the security discourse in the region.

This publication was made possible by the Kodikara Award for South Asian Strategic Studies.

Contact address:

Regional Centre for Strategic Studies
68/1, Sarasavi Lane
Colombo-08
Sri Lanka
Tel: + (94) 11-2690913, 2690914
Fax: + (94) 11-2690769
E-mail: info@rcss.org
Website: www.rcss.org

RCSS Policy Studies 53

Maritime Cooperation in South Asia

SITHARA FERNANDO

REGIONAL CENTRE FOR STRATEGIC STUDIES
COLOMBO

MANOHAR
2013

Published by
Ajay Kumar Jain *for*
Manohar Publishers & Distributors
4753/23 Ansari Road, Daryaganj
New Delhi 110 002
and
Regional Centre for Strategic Studies
68/1, Sarasavi Lane
Colombo-08
SRI LANKA
Tel: + (94) 11-2690913, 2690914; Fax: + (94) 11-2690769
E-mail: info@rcss.org
Website: www.rcss.org

First published 2013

ISBN 978-81-7304-991-0

Printed at
Salasar Imaging Systems
Delhi 110 035

Contents

Introduction

Nearly three-fourths of the earth's surface is occupied by oceans. For centuries, people have used ocean space for two main purposes: fishing and navigation. The oceans have been one of the 'global commons' beyond the jurisdiction of any single state, somewhat like the common pastures in medieval villages that were open for all villagers to use. Just as medieval villages were eventually fenced off in response to economic change, states too 'fenced off' large parts of the oceans in the 1970 as technological advances and economic changes increased the uses of the oceans. During negotiations at the third United Nations Conference on the Law of the Sea (UNCLOS III) from 1973 to 1982, the idea of allowing states to claim 200 nautical miles (NM) Exclusive Economic Zones (EEZs) in the oceans off their coasts received wide support. Under this plan, nearly one-third of the world's oceans came under national jurisdictions (Keohane and Nye 2001: 75).

Today, while the decline of sea travel and diminished dependence on self-supplied food sources has removed the maritime world from the realm of most land dwellers' everyday experiences, the sea remains a crucial domain for the resources and processes that sustain contemporary life. Since World War II, global fish catch has increased tenfold as has total tonnage shipped by the world's cargo fleet. Similarly, offshore petroleum extraction has increased rapidly since the first commercial well was sunk in 1937. Today, over 20 per cent of the world's petroleum is derived from offshore sources and the oceans present a host of other mineral extraction opportunities. Tourism promotion too has taken a leading role in many countries' development plans, and this activity frequently involves further human interaction with the sea. Biologists are turning to the sea as the next frontier for genetic and pharmacological research and, with this increased attention to marine biota, there is now heightened awareness of the fragility of marine ecosystems and the connections between the health of both marine and terrestrial environments. Combining all of the resources provided by the ocean, economists have calculated that the sea provides to humanity services valued at 21 trillion dollars, while the land provides services worth only 12 trillion dollars (Steinberg 2001: 8–9).

With this increasing usage of the sea, while military strategy has largely sought to 'use' ocean space in the interest of one country (or a group of countries) against the interest of another country (or group), the United Nations Convention on the Law of the Sea of 1982 (LOSC 1982) has sought to peacefully 'regulate the use' of ocean space in the interest of all countries (UNDOALS 2007). After acquiring the necessary number of ratifications, LOSC 1982 entered into force in 1994. Linked to LOSC 1982, and applicable to South Asia, Alam (1997) had put forward an academic proposal for the formation of a South Asian Association for Regional Cooperation (SAARC) Centre for Maritime Cooperation (CMC), with the following suggested objectives:

1. To foster maritime cooperation and dialogue among the SAARC states and promote maritime confidence and security building measures;
2. To promote adherence to the principles of the LOSC 1982, commence dialogue on the areas of LOSC 1982, which are either indefinite or not fully accepted by regional nations, and promote joint hydrographic survey efforts to assist in the observance and implementation of LOSC 1982;
3. To create a secure atmosphere and help safeguard peaceful merchant shipping of the region and examine the means for developing the procedures, which will assist in the protection of shipping within the region with increased joint activity in naval control of shipping;
4. To facilitate sustained exploitation of the resources of the sea

and identify regional hydrographic survey and oceanographic priorities and examine ways to conduct joint surveys in those waters with greatest priority;

5. To contribute to the preservation of the marine environment and provide a framework of cooperation for weather prediction; and
6. To undertake policy-oriented studies on specific regional maritime security problems and provide training in relevant aspects of maritime operations to those lacking in certain types of capability or expertise (Alam 1997: 36–7).

Given the fact that ships carry out most of the international trade, what is probably one of the best reasons for South Asia to institutionalize and engage in maritime cooperation is provided by the Agreement on South Asian Free Trade Area (SAFTA), reached in January 2004 at the 12th SAARC Summit in Islamabad, Pakistan. The framework agreement on SAFTA stipulated the reduction of customs duties on all traded goods to zero by the year 2016. After acquiring the necessary ratifications, the SAFTA Agreement came into force in January 2006 (SAARC 2012b; 2012c). However, Pakistan granted Most Favoured Nation (MFN) trade status to India only as late as November 2011 (*Daily News* 2011c). This points towards a perennial problem faced by SAARC—that of the rather unstable and crisis-prone India–Pakistan relationship. Apart from trade, SAARC cooperation has often been held hostage by the vagaries of the India–Pakistan dynamic in other areas too. That is to say, the problems in a bilateral relationship have stood in the way of regional multilateral cooperation. As a way of getting around this obstacle, this study would like to propose a bottom-up approach of building regional multilateral maritime cooperation from bilateral maritime cooperation. It is worth noting that, in the context of naval cooperation in the eastern sub-region of the Indian Ocean, Roy-Chaudhury (1998: 275) has argued that, '. . . the development and growth of a web of bilateral naval relationships could, over a period of time, be made to evolve into a loosely defined multilateral set of activities. . . .'

MARITIME ISSUES FACING SOUTH ASIA AND PROSPECTS FOR REGIONAL COOPERATION

Maritime issues facing South Asia include boundary problems, fisheries conflicts, non-military/non-traditional security threats and environmental problems. The India–Pakistan maritime boundary is undemarcated due to the dispute over Sir Creek, which creates a problem in finding a land terminus for the maritime boundary. While the India–Sri Lanka maritime boundary was demarcated and legally laid to rest by the 1974 and 1976 agreements between the two countries, as recently as May/June 2011, the Chief Minister of Tamil Nadu J. Jayalalithaa has claimed a right for Tamil Nadu fishermen to fish in waters around the island of Kachchativu, which falls on the Sri Lankan side of the maritime boundary. The India–Bangladesh maritime boundary too is undemarcated due to differences in the principles by which it is to be demarcated, as well as disputed sovereignty over a small island known as New Moore or Purbasha in India and South Talpatty in Bangladesh. Even as bilateral negotiations should doubtless proceed in all three cases, arriving at a common regional interpretation of LOSC 1982 could also go some way towards resolving these problems.

Related to the boundary problems as well as to the nature of fishing itself, where fish do not respect national boundaries, there is the issue of fishermen unlawfully crossing over into the maritime territories of the neighbouring country, in pursuit of their livelihoods. This problem exists between India and each of the South Asian countries mentioned above—Pakistan, Sri Lanka, and Bangladesh. Several measures can be taken to deal with this problem. The technology of vessel monitoring systems can be used to alert fishermen through signals when they are straying over into another country's territory. Joint fisheries zones can be established where fishermen from different countries can fish. A certain number of fishing licences could also be granted by each country to fishermen from other countries. Measures can also be put in place, in recognition of the livelihood aspect of the issue, to deal with bonafide fishermen who do cross over into another country's territory in as humane a manner as possible. While many of these measures can be implemented bilaterally, some degree of multilateralization could also be helpful given the highly migratory nature of fish stocks.

The non-military/non-traditional maritime security threats facing South Asia include maritime terrorism and smuggling. While the Liberation Tigers of Tamil Elam (LTTE), which constituted a grave threat to South Asian maritime security for many years, is no longer a military force, rump elements are still active. The connection between terrorism and maritime security was most forcefully brought to our attention by the maritime dimension of the terrorist attacks on Mumbai in November 2008. The smuggling of women and children from Bangladesh into India and Pakistan is widespread. Meanwhile, rump elements of the LTTE are reported to be involved in the smuggling of Sri Lankan Tamil refugees from India to countries such as Australia and Canada. The port of Chittagong in Bangladesh is well known as a major route for smuggling of arms to terrorists operating in north-east India. To deal with this complex of non-military/non-traditional threats, a regional network of maritime surveillance and reconnaissance systems, including multilateral joint sea and air patrols and radars, can be contemplated.

For the five maritime nations of South Asia—India, Pakistan, Sri Lanka, Bangladesh, and The Maldives—the coastal areas represent a crucial part of the life support system in the region. Coastal areas are also significant in that millions of people in South Asia live in coastal areas and depend on coastal/marine resources for their livelihoods. These areas also contribute towards a major part of these nations' economies. The South Asian region has extensive mangrove areas and some of the world's least disturbed coral reefs. However, these coastal/marine ecosystems are subjected to increasing exploitation and other anthropogenic disturbances. At the same time, climate change, with its attendant sea level rise, is a major challenge for these South Asian countries that face large climatic variability and enhanced risks from climate change. Hence, sustainable management of coastal and marine resources has become a vital issue for these countries, and there is a need to integrate environmental management into their development planning. In this respect, the SAARC Coastal Zone Management Centre (SCZMC) inaugurated in 2005 plays an important role, particularly in facilitating experience sharing among member countries in coastal zone management (CZM) and promoting the concept of integrated coastal zone management (ICZM) (SCZMC 2011a).

REVIEW OF LITERATURE

Pinto (1992) is highly useful for analysing the contribution of LOSC 1982 to maritime security in terms of naval mobility in time of peace; the theme of reservation for 'peaceful purposes'; proliferation of peaceful uses; and the system for settling disputes. Given the fact that Articles 98, 100, 108, 192, 194, 276 and 277 of LOSC 1982 encourage regional cooperation in maritime affairs, Pinto's contribution can be regarded as a useful overall framework within which to think of maritime security cooperation in South Asia. Given the emerging regionalization of the South Asian economy, intra-South Asia shipping traffic is bound to increase in the near future. In this context, Graham's (2006) conceptual analysis of sea lines of communication (SLOC)[1]/sea lanes is of much

[1] First, the two phrases 'sea lines of communication' and 'sea lanes of communication' are both often abbreviated to the acronym SLOC. The term 'line' indicates the shortest possible distance between two points, while the term 'lane' indicates a transport route. Since the functional referent of both 'lane' and 'communication' in this context is transport, the term 'communication' in the phrase 'sea lanes of communication' is rendered redundant. Therefore it is possible to argue that the correct usage would be 'sea lines of communication' and 'sea lanes'. Hence the acronym SLOC should denote only the abbreviation of the phrase 'sea lines of communication'. Second, SLOC refers to one's own 'lines of communication' at sea, that is to say a nation's, an alliance's, or a coalition's 'lines of communication' at sea. Therefore, while it may make sense to refer to the security of one's own SLOC, it does not make sense to refer to regional SLOC security, or international SLOC security, unless this involves a separation of one's own SLOC from those of others, and the according of recognition and immunity to each other's SLOC, in a particular region, or among two or more nations, alliances, or coalitions. At the same time, it is important to keep in mind that one can refer to a nation's, an alliance's, or a coalition's 'sea lanes'. That is to say, while the phrase 'sea lines of communication' is applicable only in a limited context, the phrase 'sea lanes' is

use. For Graham, together with military strategy and economics, SLOC also involves international law, and LOSC 1982 may have reinforced an order-based institutionalized approach to establishing a common legal framework that recognizes the sovereignty claims of coastal states while upholding rights of navigation through international straits and offshore areas of all states.

While a great deal of attention has been devoted to regional maritime cooperation by the Association of Southeast Asian Nations (ASEAN) Regional Forum, also called ARF, through its Track II initiative the Council for Security Cooperation in the Asia-Pacific (CSCAP), there has been comparatively little attention to maritime cooperation in South Asia, with the sole exception of Alam (1997). While nothing much appears to have come out directly from Alam's academic proposal, it gives us a fairly comprehensive idea of what South Asian maritime cooperation could look like and how we can operationalize it.

However, in the last ten years or so, numerous publications on India–Pakistan and India–Sri Lanka maritime cooperation have been produced. Siddiqa-Agha (2000) advocates a confidence building approach that can alter the existing hostile images and perceptions between the Indian and Pakistani navies. She proposes a five-step model comprising (1) the Signalling Stage to initiate communication between the two navies; (2) the Warming-Up Stage to build confidence through non-military joint activity; (3) the Handshake Stage to build confidence between the two navies through military joint activity; (4) the Problem-Solving Stage to resolve outstanding disputes; and (5) the Final Nod Stage to initiate naval arms control. She envisions Track II initiatives involving senior retired naval officers of India and Pakistan playing an important role in the early stages of the confidence building model. Building on Siddiqa-Agha's work, Ansari and Vohra (2003) argue that maritime issues of mutual concern provide a strong

more broadly applicable. This is perhaps what makes it possible for the two phrases 'sea lines of communication' and 'sea lanes' to be used interchangeably. Third, it is important to keep in mind that a 'sea line of communication' on a map represents a 'sea lane' in the real world. See the section on 'Sea Lines of Communication/Sea Lanes' for further elaboration.

foundation for more far-reaching confidence building measures (CBMs) between India and Pakistan on land in the long term, while addressing immediate security, economic and humanitarian needs at sea in the short term. They focus on technology as a valuable tool to build confidence between states having a low level of initial trust, as in the case of India and Pakistan. They advocate a number of technical CBMs as well as political recommendations regarding the following issues: delimitation of the maritime boundary between India and Pakistan and its relationship to the Sir Creek dispute; restoration of full shipping links and the security of ports and cargos; fishing within disputed areas and resolution of issues relating to arrest and repatriation of fishermen from both sides; and naval and maritime agency interaction and possibilities for cooperation. Ghosh (2008) critically examines the existing CBMs in the maritime field between India and Pakistan, and proposes a set of further measures.

Meanwhile, Raju and Keethaponcalan's (2006) study on maritime cooperation between India and Sri Lanka examines the following issues: (1) security concerns of India and Sri Lanka; (2) the Indian Ocean as a Zone of Peace (IOZP) initiative; (3) the Kachchativu issue; (4) fishermen's problems; (5) the proposed land bridge between India and Sri Lanka; (6) the Sethusamudram Shipping Canal Project; (7) the threat from the LTTE; (8) the Tamil refugee problem; (9) economic cooperation; and (10) energy cooperation. While some of these issues, such as the proposed land bridge and the Sethusamudram project have faded into the background, other issues such as the fishermen's problems and economic cooperation are still relevant. The LTTE issue also remains relevant, though in an altered form. The issues covered in Vohra and Srivatsan (2008)—an edited collection of papers presented at what might be called a Track II forum on India–Sri Lanka maritime cooperation organized by the National Maritime Foundation (NMF) in New Delhi in December 2006—include the overall political outlook for India–Sri Lanka maritime cooperation, prospects for cooperation in offshore oil and gas development and marine resource exploitation; environment; and security. This study will draw on this literature on India–Pakistan and India–Sri Lanka maritime cooperation with a view towards contributing to the evolving agenda for South Asian multilateral maritime cooperation.

RATIONALIZATION FOR CHAPTERIZATION

Currently, the maritime issues facing South Asia include boundary problems, fisheries conflicts, non-military/non-traditional security threats and environmental problems. This study seeks to facilitate solutions of these problems through regional cooperation. Theorizing of the maritime domain tends to be dominated by military strategic thinkers such as Alfred Thayer Mahan, best known for his identification of the six elements of sea power: (1) geographic position; (2) physical conformation (including natural resources and climate); (3) extent of territory; (4) population; (5) character of the people; and (6) character of the government (Tangredi 2002). However, the point to note about thinkers such as Mahan is that they theorized from the perspective of the interests of a particular country, in Mahan's case the US. Those who follow Mahan's thinking around the world tend to advocate the building up of the navies of their respective countries without regard to the security dilemma created in a situation in which several countries are building up their navies at the same time. On the other hand, LOSC 1982 is imbibed with a more universalist perspective that takes into account the interests of as many countries as possible, providing a basis not only for global maritime cooperation but also for regional maritime cooperation. Therefore, in the face of the dominance of military strategic thinking in the maritime domain, this study seeks to base South Asian maritime cooperation on LOSC 1982. It posits the emerging regionalization of the South Asian economy under the SAFTA Agreement as providing the most fundamental rationale for initiating maritime cooperation under SAARC. Accordingly, the consideration of the maritime dimension of international law and the concept of SLOC/sea lanes in Chapter One provides a theoretical framework for facilitating South Asian maritime cooperation. The research problem that this study seeks to address is the issue of institutionalization of South Asian maritime cooperation.

Given the range of maritime problems facing the region, this is an issue that should be addressed in a timely manner. Thus, Chapter Two considers Alam's academic proposal for the establishment of a SAARC CMC and related developments that have taken place till the time of writing. Given the slow progress in institutionalizing maritime cooperation within SAARC, Chapter Two also considers the possibility of institutionalizing South Asian maritime cooperation independently of SAARC yet complementary to it. In international relations literature, bilateral and multilateral relations tend to be considered as distinct and separate spheres of activity, ignoring the fact that often problems in a bilateral relationship can stand in the way of the progress of a multilateral process. One of the best examples of this occurrence is the case of India–Pakistan bilateral problems preventing the progress of SAARC. Therefore, Chapter Three examines efforts at India–Pakistan and India–Sri Lanka bilateral maritime cooperation, seeking to build South Asian maritime cooperation from the bottom up, based on these two sets of bilateral relationships.

Before proceeding to Chapter One, a few words must be said about the interests of extra-regional and regional powers in maritime security in South Asia and the overall prospects for South Asian maritime cooperation. The sea lane running just off South Asia is a major artery of world trade and countries in Western Europe, East Asia and North America have an interest in its security. The security of this sea lane is particularly vital to China, Japan and South Korea, which are highly dependent on West Asian/Middle Eastern oil transported along it. The US claims to have been facilitating freedom of navigation on the 'high seas', including in the Indian Ocean. While in recent years the US has been burdened with an ailing economy and, as a consequence, has had to endure cuts in defence expenditure, the United States Navy (USN) is still the most powerful navy in the Indian Ocean. However, due to its relative decline, it is looking for allies in the region, which can shoulder a greater share of the burden of securing sea lanes. In this respect, India with its overwhelming geographic advantage in the Indian Ocean and its growing naval and maritime capabilities is well positioned to play this role and to assume some sort of a coleadership position. However, in doing so, India will have to take cognizance of the concerns about 'Indian hegemony' among its neighbours in South Asia, and work diplomatically to dispel such concerns. While given the international character of the 'high sea' in accordance with LOSC 1982, any prospective institution for South Asian maritime cooperation must involve a mechanism for the participation of extra-regional countries, a significant portion of the responsibility of ensuring maritime security in the region must lie with the countries of the region. Whether the South Asian countries will in fact be able to get their act together and develop an institution for maritime cooperation could depend on the fate of India's efforts at bilateral maritime cooperation with other South Asian countries. In addition, whether SAARC will begin to give more attention to the issue of maritime security could depend on the fate of an official governmental proposal by The Maldives to develop principles of modern law relating to maritime security and piracy tabled at the 33rd session of the SAARC Council of Ministers in February 2011.

CHAPTER ONE

International Maritime Cooperation: Some Theoretical Perspectives

INTRODUCTION

This chapter will focus on two aspects of international maritime cooperation. First, it will explore the maritime dimension of international law. Pinto (1992: 9–10) has noted:

> It was the activities of merchantmen and naval vessels that first inspired a movement in the direction of clarifying or developing rules to govern conduct among nations. Among those nations on whom economic and political power conferred the capacity to influence emerging legal concepts, the use of the sea to carry on trade, as well as for defence and other military purposes, was part of the natural order of things, and development of the law of the sea throughout most of history, centred on transport, transit and naval activity. . . . While the nineteenth century did see the conclusion of international agreements regulating fishing on the high sea, it was only about the middle of the twentieth century that there appears evidence of a shift from preoccupation with the rules governing navigation and the military uses of the sea to those concerned with exploration for and exploitation of living and non-living marine resources.

Second, it will examine the link between international trade and shipping through the concept of SLOC/sea lanes. While relatively recent developments in information and communication technology have enabled buyers and sellers to enter into transactions within seconds in cyberspace, if they are separated by a large physical distance and if the transaction involves a large volume of goods, chances are that they will still be dependent on maritime transport for the actual completion of their transaction. Therefore, the first and second sections of this chapter will focus on the maritime dimension of international law and SLOC/sea lanes, respectively. The research problem this study seeks to address is the issue of institutionalization of maritime cooperation in South Asia, and it seeks to do so in accordance with LOSC 1982. It also posits the emerging regionalization of the South Asian economy under the SAFTA agreement as providing the most fundamental rationale for South Asian maritime cooperation, and given that ships transport most of international trade the concept of SLOC/sea lanes merits consideration in this context.

THE MARITIME DIMENSION OF INTERNATIONAL LAW

Around 1500 BC, the Phoenicians had founded a colony on the small Aegean island known as Rhodes at the crossroads of maritime traffic in the eastern Mediterranean. Due to its strategic position between Egypt, Cyprus, the Syrian and Phoenician coasts and the world of the Greek cities, Rhodes emerged as an important intermediary point between Greece and the Orient and became the foremost commercial centre in the Mediterranean. It also fulfilled the role of a policeman of both Mediterranean and international trade, which resulted in a constant battle against pirates. Around the third or second century BC, Rhodes codified the commercial practices of the time in the form of Rhodesian sea law, an act some consider to have laid the foundation of modern maritime jurisprudence. Due to its intellectual eminence, Rhodian sea law, which created several maritime codes and assumed a binding character freely recognized by the seagoing states of the Mediterranean, is said to have taken precedence in the Mediterranean. Later, it is said to have influenced the Byzantine Empire and even Roman law. The Rhodian code seems to have included regulations regarding the partnership, joint adventures, charter parties and bills of lading. It is said to have established standards of behaviour of the passengers on board and liability of the commander or seaman in cases of dereliction of duty. This sea law was copied and handed down through the centuries in this form. Even in the Middle Ages, it guided the maritime and commercial adventures of European merchants (Anand 1983: 10–11).

Based on principles outlined by Hugo Grotius in the seventeenth century, especially in his treatise *Mare Librum*, much of the world's sea and ocean space was regarded as the 'high sea' in which all states enjoyed equal freedom of navigation rights. From then till the mid-twentieth century, in demarcating their 'territorial waters', most states adhered to a 'three-mile limit'. However, a dramatic shift in the legal status of seas and oceans was initiated in the mid-twentieth century by the dynamic of 'coastal states', many of which were, on the one hand, newly-decolonized states seeking to assert and extend their 'sovereignty' beyond the three-mile limit and, on the other, 'Western maritime states' seeking to preserve freedom of navigation and maximize their access to marine resources in the water column and seabed. The need to negotiate a compromise between the interests of 'coastal states' and 'maritime states' led to UNCLOS I, II, III concluding in 1958, 1968, 1982, respectively (Graham 2006: 51). The debate between 'coastal states' seeking to extend their sovereignty out to sea and 'maritime states' seeking to preserve freedom of navigation and maximize their access to marine resources can be seen as a resurgence of the debate between the principles of *mare clausum* (closed sea) and *mare librum* (free sea) that took place in Europe following the publication of Grotius' treatise (Anand 1983: 77–88, 95–7, 99–106).

LOSC 1982 does not deal directly with military uses of the seas. The sort of international agreements that deal directly with military issues are those concerning 'disarmament' and 'arms control'. Pinto (1992) has examined the contribution of LOSC 1982 to maritime security in terms of naval mobility in time of peace; the theme of reservation for 'peaceful purposes'; proliferation of peaceful uses; and the system for settling disputes.

The overt or covert projection of naval power at will attained the status of an attribute of state sovereignty during the formative stages of international law. The risk of particular coastal states restricting the movement of foreign navies introduces an element of uncertainty into such power projection. An international treaty regulating naval mobility in time of peace reduces such uncertainty.

While the capabilities of states for naval power projection differ, an agreed and uniformly applicable framework regulating such activity is of relative value to the maritime security of all states. Moreover, the major maritime powers had been willing to recognize the rights over marine resources by not so powerful coastal states and by 'mankind as a whole' in exchange for rights of passage and rights to conduct other naval operations. Provisions of the convention that deal with this issue are those that accord warships a special status and immunity, and those that limit by reference to specified zones, the seaward extension of coastal state jurisdiction while ensuring, as far as possible, freedom of warships and other ships on 'government non-commercial service' to traverse those zones and to conduct other lawful activities within them (Pinto 1992: 12–13).

On the high seas and the subjacent sea-bed, warships and other ships owned or operated by a state and used only on government non-commercial service have 'complete immunity' from the jurisdiction of any state other than the flag state. In the EEZs, on the continental shelf, and in areas subject to coastal state sovereignty in which warships have a right of passage (such as the territorial sea, the contiguous zone, straits used for international navigation and archipelagic waters), they are not immune from the 'legislative jurisdiction' of the coastal state. While such a ship's flag state also has concurrent legislative authority, it is the flag state alone that has 'enforcement jurisdiction' over it. Therefore, if such a ship does not comply with the laws and regulations of a coastal state concerning 'innocent passage' through the territorial sea and disregards a request for compliance therewith, the coastal state is, in principle, entitled to do no more than require it to leave the territorial sea immediately. If such a ship were to fail to comply during 'transit passage' through straits used for international navigation with the coastal state's navigational safety regulations, and cause damage, it would engage the 'international responsibility' of the flag state. Immunity from national jurisdiction does not imply immunity from international responsibility. The institutional mechanisms through which a flag state may be held to be responsible by a coastal state are diplomatic channels and agreed dispute settlement methods (Pinto 1992: 13–15).

The scope of a coastal state's right to enact and to enforce laws in adjacent 'marine zones' diminishes as the distance from its shores increases. Its right in 'internal waters', 'archipelagic waters' and in the 'territorial sea' reflects its sovereignty over those zones and arises out of recognition of the primacy of its interests, both in security and marine resources. Its jurisdiction in the 'contiguous zone' is limited to specified law enforcement purposes, while jurisdiction over the EEZ and the continental shelf are acknowledged primarily for resource exploitation purposes. The convention's provisions for maintaining naval mobility reflect a negotiated balance between the interests of coastal states in ensuring their security from foreign interference from the sea as well as in marine resources, and the interests of all states in the use of the sea for commercial and military transport. There are several 'regimes', which govern naval mobility within the different marine zones: (1) consent of the coastal state; (2) innocent passage; (3) transit passage; (4) mixed regimes and treaty regimes in straights used for international navigation; (5) regimes applicable in archipelagic waters; (6) freedom of navigation and overflight in EEZs; (7) regime of the continental shelf; (8) freedom of the high seas; and (9) regime governing the seabed and ocean floor and the subsoil thereof beyond the limits of national jurisdiction (Pinto 1992: 16–31).

The theme of reservation of the sea for 'peaceful purposes' and 'peaceful use' is emphasized in several contexts, and interpretation of the theme is relevant to determining the overall effect of the convention on maritime security. The preamble declares that the convention should be an 'important contribution to the maintenance of peace', that it should 'promote the peaceful uses of the seas and oceans', and that the codification and progressive development of the law of the sea achieved in the convention would 'contribute to the strengthening of peace, security, cooperation and friendly relations among all nations. . . .' Article 88 contains the unqualified assertion 'the high seas shall be reserved for peaceful purposes'. Article 58(2) applies the theme to the EEZ. The continental shelf of a state lying beyond its EEZ would be considered subject to the regime of the high sea and thus also subject to the reservation. With regard to the area of the sea-bed and the ocean floor beyond the limits of national jurisdiction Article 141 states: 'The Area shall be open to use exclusively for peaceful purposes by all states. . . .' The principles governing freedom of marine scientific research generally, Article 240(a), and with respect to the Area, Article 143, and the erection of research installations, Article 147(2)(d), also contain restrictions to use for peaceful purposes. Other provisions of the convention, instead of requiring that a particular maritime activity be carried out for peaceful purposes, prohibit the 'threat or use of force'. Article 301 states the prohibition in its most general form under the heading 'peaceful uses of the seas': 'In exercising their rights and performing their duties under this Convention, States Parties shall refrain from any threat or use of force against the territorial integrity or political independence of any state, or in any other manner inconsistent with the principles of international law embodied in the Charter of the United Nations.' Within Article 19, sub-paragraph 2(a) imposes the obligation to refrain from the threat or use of force on ships in innocent passage through the territorial sea to safeguard the security of coastal states. Article 39 sub-paragraph 1(b) imposes the same obligation on ships in transit passage through straits used for international navigation to safeguard the security of states bordering such straits (Pinto 1992: 31–2).

The phrase '. . . principles of international law embodied in the Charter of the United Nations' in Article 301 recalls the lawfulness of the use of force in accordance with Chapter VII of the UN Charter, in which Article 51 is on the 'right of self-defence'. Since times immemorial, the sea has been used as a medium by all countries for fortification and defence of their territories; the convention could not have intended to prohibit the use of the sea for military purposes of any kind. The provisions for 'peaceful use' and the prohibition of 'threat or use of force' express the aspiration of all states party to the convention to accord some priority to maintaining peace on the seas and reserving them 'as far as possible' for peaceful use (Pinto 1992: 32, 34–5).

The convention's provisions on reservation for 'peaceful purposes', without precedent in any earlier multilateral agreements on the law of the sea, should be seen as forming the foundation of its regulatory and institutional framework aimed at promoting the exploration, exploitation, conservation, and management of marine resources in an equitable, rational, and sustainable manner. These activities are facilitated by the maintenance of peace at sea. The implementation of the convention's numerous provisions on resource management and conservation are, in turn, likely to lead in the long run to a gradual reduction of military activity at sea. Elaborates Pinto (1992):

> As the need for sea-bed minerals foreseen earlier becomes a reality, and prospecting and mining operations commence in areas of the ocean floor from the Indian Ocean to the Pacific, under the supervision of the International Sea-bed Authority; as living resource management measures provided for under the Convention, administered by competent regional and international organizations in partnership with coastal states, result in a substantial widening of participants in the harvesting of optimum sustainable yields, and the Convention's marine technology transfer provisions succeed in augmenting the harvesting capacities of many states not currently engaged in intensive fishing efforts; and as the provisions preventing marine pollution and promoting marine scientific research bring about the active participation of increasing numbers of scientists, technicians and administrators from around the world, the Convention would have so multiplied the variety, frequency and geographical incidence of marine resource-related activity that pressures generated through the obligation to accommodate these proliferating peaceful uses, could not but result in significantly reducing both the need and the scope for military activity at sea, and would then have accomplished that aim in the most natural and effective manner.

However, the proliferation of peaceful uses of the sea can also increase the likelihood and frequency of disputes. As such usage of the sea increases, the chances and instances of disputes arising over issues such as the establishment of maritime boundaries in areas of high resource potential will also increase, hence the importance of the convention's system for settling disputes. A substantial degree of flexibility is also built into the system. Part XV of the convention offers a wide array of settlement mechanisms provided for in Article 33 Paragraph 1 of the UN Charter. A dispute can be submitted for resolution under some other global, regional, or bilateral treaty. If the parties to a dispute are unable to reach a settlement by a method chosen by themselves, the convention first directs them to 'procedures not entailing binding decisions' such as, under Article 283 to exchange views regarding settlement by negotiation or other means, and under Article 284 to consider upon the request of one party implementing the conciliation procedures prescribed in Annex V of the convention. If no settlement has been reached through such preliminary initiatives, parties to a dispute are directed to 'compulsory procedures entailing binding decisions' set forth or referred to in Section 2 of Part XV. On signing, ratifying or acceding to the convention, a state may make a formal declaration choosing one or more of four mechanisms as the means by which its disputes concerning the interpretation or application of the convention would be settled. These four mechanisms are: (1) the International Tribunal for the Law of the Sea functioning in accordance with Annex VI; (2) the International Court of Justice; (3) an arbitral tribunal constituted in accordance with Annex VII; and (4) a special tribunal for specified disputes of a technical nature constituted in accordance with Annex VIII. In recognition of the possibility that some disputes can be politically sensitive there are 'limitations on the applicability of procedures entailing binding decisions' and an 'option to exclude certain disputes altogether from the application of procedures entailing binding decisions' (Pinto 1992: 37–9).

Pinto (1992: 51–2) notes that the convention has been criticized for ambiguity in some of its provisions. According to him, these provisions deal with politically sensitive situations relating to state security concerning which the conference was not able to adopt clear rules acceptable both to coastal states and naval powers, which would reflect a 'balance of interests' between them. These provisions apply to situations of lack of trust between states, situations in which CBMs can be most helpful. He argues that a link can be drawn between CBMs as 'voluntary demonstrations of benign intent' and Article 300 of the convention on 'good faith and abuse of rights', which states that 'States' Parties shall fulfil in good faith the obligations assumed under this Convention and shall exercise rights, jurisdiction and freedoms recognized in this convention in a manner which would not constitute an abuse of right'.

SEA LINES OF COMMUNICATION/SEA LANES

Graham (2006: 34–62) provides a detailed analysis of the concept of SLOC. According to him, the term 'sea lines of communication' originates from an analogy drawn between overland lines of supply such as the fixed infrastructure of roads and railways used by armies to connect forces at the front with bases and production centres in the rear. These require the control or at least the neutrality of the surrounding territory. The definition of lines of communication at sea is more relative due to the difference in the properties of water and land. He also argues that the overlapping use of terms such as 'chokepoints', 'sea lanes', 'strategic waterways', 'trade routes', 'focal areas', 'approaches' and so on risk conflating the principles of naval strategy with those governing maritime economics. He also points out that while, on the one hand, sea space can be a barrier to the movement of people and separation by a large body of water can be an advantage against a large-scale invasion by ground forces, on the other, the relative efficiency of waterborne transportation compared with overland transportation can be an advantage in projecting military power and conducting trade (Graham 2006: 35–7).

Prominent naval and maritime strategic thinkers Mahan and Julian Corbett have both acknowledged the importance of trade routes at sea and merchant shipping from the viewpoint of military strategy. Mahan differentiated functionally between 'lines of communication' for military ventures and 'lines of travel' for trade. Corbett categorized maritime communications into those required by the belligerents' fleets for supply of fuel, stores, and ammunition; those between an army overseas and its home base; those servicing the resource needs of the belligerents' home bases; and those connecting the belligerents' overseas bases. Corbett argued that 'focal areas' and 'terminals' of trade routes were the areas in which merchant shipping was most vulnerable, and advocated 'flotilla guards' (small fleets) to defend these in conjunction with blockades of an adversary's ports. As far as those parts of trade routes in the 'open sea' were concerned, Corbett had advocated 'naval patrol' rather than 'convoys' (groups of merchant ships escorted by naval ships). However, both Mahan and Corbett thought that 'commerce warfare' (*guerre de course*, literally 'war of the chase') could not be decisive by itself and that it was marginal within naval strategy. Corbett had thought of commerce warfare as the non-lethal seizure of merchant ships. The effectiveness of the submarine in commerce warfare during World War I, however, was based on the lethal targeting of merchant ships (Graham 2006: 35–9).

In 'attrition-based conflict', industrial capacity and economic stamina can be decisive factors. While Raoul Castex acknowledged that in 'total war', the distinction between economic and military factors might be less marked, he argued that a distinction could be drawn between maritime communications in times of peace and in times of war. Maritime communication in times of war would involve those required to sustain a war economy, those requiring forces to be moved and those fulfilling internal communications under certain geographic conditions. He stressed the importance of national geography, population and distribution of resources (energy, raw materials, food) as factors influencing the different extents to which a disruption of seaborne trade would affect states. By the 1920s, oil had begun replacing coal as the primary 'bunker fuel' for most major navies, making it one of the most important 'strategic commodities'. In a conflict in which economic strength can be decisive, 'accessory concerns' such as navy–transport bureau relations, stockpiling and austerity measures to limit import demand were recognized by Castex as integral to an overall national effort. While he too held that commerce war could not be decisive by itself, he did recognize the potential of the submarine and the aeroplane to erode the dominance of surface fleets in naval warfare, and was a keen proponent of the submarine. As a practitioner of anti-submarine warfare (ASW), with regard to measures to protect shipping against submarines, he considered 'convoy' to be superior to arming, diverting or independently routing merchant ships, and rejected the concept of patrolled areas as misconceived. He argued that 'convoy' minimized losses, returned the initiative to the defence by maximizing the potential for counter-attack, and maintained the focus on defending 'the objects themselves rather than space' (Graham 2006: 39–40).

Bernard Brodie too recognized that, in 'total war', the outcome depended on industrial capacity to compensate for shipping losses as much as on naval strategy. Brodie identified three types of defensive cover for shipping: general cover, evasive routing, and direct protection. General cover refers to the indirect protection conferred through command of the sea secured through a superior naval force, which is able to destroy or neutralize a hostile fleet. Evasive routing is the most basic form of protection against a sub-surface or air attack for merchant shipping, except near terminals where concentration is unavoidable. Lone ships on the usual peacetime routes were the most vulnerable to merchant raiders. Of the strategies aimed at direct protection, convoy presented merchant ships with greater overall security than single sailings (Graham 2006: 41).

According to Graham (2006: 41–2) arguments made during World Wars I and II against the use of convoy included the observation that 'it is dull and unspectacular work', that it is logistically difficult to organize and tactically flawed since it presents a concentrated target limited in speed to the speed of the slowest vessels in the group, and that it is a purely defensive form of warfare. Arguments made for the use of convoy included the facts that it is only marginally easier to detect than single ships, that it offers the most effective means of counter-attack, and that concentration of merchant shipping in convoy present the most efficient means to allocate limited resources for their protection. Graham argues that in comparison with 'patrolled sea lanes', the main strength of 'convoying' is that it protects the ships themselves rather than just the sea lanes.

In the context of 'total war', such as that which occurred in the first half of the twentieth century, Graham (2006: 42–3) identifies numerous general principles pertaining to SLOC security. First, in the face of sustained military pressure, convoy is the best method for the defence of shipping. Second, if trans-oceanic

SLOC and shipping are well defended, they can be a medium through which power in the form of naval, air and ground forces are projected inter-continentally, and the means through which war economies are sustained. Third, maritime powers, which are import-dependent, would be the most vulnerable to the blockade of merchant shipping, which will quickly starve their industry of the resources needed to maintain a sustained war effort. Fourth, in the long run, a blockade can be effective in degrading the fighting power of even relatively autarkic continental powers. Fifth, counter-blockade and anti-shipping campaigns led by submarines hold the potential of being decisive and can yield results 'out of all proportion to the resources invested'.

In the second half of the twentieth century, during the Cold War, the emergence of nuclear weapons made sustained and intense naval warfare such as that which occurred in the immediately preceding era of 'total war' unlikely. In 1951, the Radford-Collins Naval Control of Shipping Agreement (NCS) was signed. It involved the US, Great Britain, Australia and New Zealand dividing the Pacific Ocean into geographical zones of responsibility for the protection of merchant shipping through measures such as convoying, safe routing and exchange of weather information, ASW, search and rescue (SAR), and surveillance. Surveillance was the subject of another agreement in 1978. Organizations for the NCS, spanning activities such as sailing authorization, route selection, convoy organization, tactical diversions and movement reportage were maintained, even after the collapse of the Soviet Union, by the US and allies such as Australia and Singapore, manned largely by naval reservists. In the late 1980s, Vice Admiral J. Blouin (1989: 56–8) outlined four measures for securing key Pacific SLOC: (1) convoy, (2) independent sailings, (3) defended lanes, and (4) offensive operations. In this context, the notion of patrolled SLOC was revived as an 'expansion of the convoy concept'. According to Vice Admiral Blouin,

> A protected or defended lane would involve sanitizing a geographical area against the submarine threat, followed by the installation of a barrier or protected perimeter to provide for penetration warning. . . . Protective forces would be positioned along a transit route. Each unit of

the protective force would be assigned an area of responsibility, the size of which depended upon the speed and sensors of the protective platform, perceived threat, environmental conditions and weapons involved.

The credibility of this revival of the idea of patrolled lanes was based on advances made since 1945 in ASW technology, drawing on the combined resources of air- and sea-based patrol units and a global remote surveillance infrastructure, based on a network of sound surveillance sonar system (SOSUS), sea-bed acoustic arrays, land-based high-frequency radio detection nets and dedicated naval reconnaissance satellites, providing comprehensive optical, infra-red and signals-intelligence coverage of the oceans. Despite such technical advances, the idea of patrolled SLOC continued to be criticized as too abstract a concept. A proposal to establish a private study group to examine the issue of SLOC security in the Asia-Pacific region in 1979 led to the inauguration of a series of bi-annual international conferences in 1982. Co-organized by the US, Japan, South Korea, Australia, China, Taiwan and several member states of the Association of South East Asian Nations (ASEAN), these conferences were attended by politicians, defence officials, serving military officers and representatives from shipping firms and other maritime industries. By the end of the Cold War, the conference agenda had evolved into three main objectives: (1) to arrive at a mutual understanding of SLOC defence; (2) to agree upon the methods of SLOC defence and its necessity; and (3) to implement practicable cooperation for SLOC defence and burden sharing (Graham 2006: 43–5).

With the end of the Cold War, the military-focused paradigm of SLOC security based on great power conflict and defence of 'freedom of navigation' on the high seas gave way to a more comprehensive agenda, incorporating political–legal and non-military issues, such as expanding maritime sovereignty claims under LOSC 1982, environmental problems and general issues concerning the safety of shipping. The scope of maritime threats was also broadened to include non-state actors involved in terrorism and piracy (Graham 2006: 46).

The existing maritime transport industry has become so internationalized that a ship's registry, owner, insurer, crew and cargo can each be from a different country. This process, which has occurred as a result of increased liberalization and commercial pressures to drive down ship operators' costs, can have strategic consequences. The dwindling of national fleets can undermine state security as the dependability of international shipping firms in times of crisis can be doubtful and governments may be unable to legally compel them to sail. It can also complicate the option of blockade by raising political costs to unacceptable levels. Coulter (1997) argues that there is a need to distinguish between military principles and market principles governing contemporary maritime transportation, particularly in relation to maritime chokepoints. While military deployments may need to be made via the most direct route in the quickest possible time, the economics of navigational access through chokepoints operates under market-based rules, which grant the system considerable flexibility to cope with the most localized obstructions. Such obstructions can be circumvented without incurring prohibitive add-on costs as long as alternative routes are available, and spare shipping and port-handling capacities exist. Therefore, chokepoints are not essential to the free flow of seaborne commerce, reflecting the fact that the choice of route is a function of market conditions. However, he acknowledges that the chokepoint at the Strait of Hormuz could be a possible exception, given its monopoly over access to oil terminals in the Persian Gulf. Coulter (1998: 135–45) further points out that the upscaling trend in the container shipping funnels world trade via a small number of 'hub ports' (capable of handling vessels with a capacity of 5,000 twenty-foot equivalent units (TEU) or above) is concentrated in East Asia, and that these could be the points at which the maritime transportation system is currently most vulnerable. There is also the issue of marine insurance. If insurance firms sharply increase premiums on traffic to certain areas considered to be volatile or extend 'exclusion zones' to those areas withdrawing insurance cover altogether, shipping firms may be unwilling or even unable to operate in those areas (Graham 2006: 48–50).

Along with military strategy and economics, SLOC also involves international law. While LOSC 1982, which entered into force in 1994, may have reinforced an order-based institutionalized approach to establishing a common legal framework that recognizes the sovereignty claims of coastal states while upholding rights of navigation through international straits and offshore areas, it may also have created a framework for 'creeping jurisdiction' that could lead to new restrictions on passage or tolls being levied on heavily used waterways. Most rights of navigation concerns relate to naval vessels and overflight rights (Graham 2006: 51–2).

MARITIME TERRORISM

Terrorism-at-sea can take the form of attacks on ships or vessels being used to deliver concealed weapons of mass destruction. Such attacks have the potential to inflict widespread damage if they take place on a ship carrying hazardous cargo or at an important location in the maritime transportation system such as a major port or strait. Terrorists can also resort to robbing ships, which is where the line between terrorism-at-sea and piracy can get blurred. They can also operate their own ships for smuggling arms, ammunition, and supplies. Hijacking and hostage taking by such groups can also be carried out at sea. Concerned international organizations and governments have initiated a number of measures to combat terrorism-at-sea. The International Maritime Bureau (IMB) has recommended that designated sea lanes used by tankers be declared 'no-go' areas for unauthorized craft, and for this imposition to be enforced by naval and police patrols. The Container Security Initiative (CSI) of the US requires designated port authorities to report, to US Customs, the contents of containers 24 hours before the ship's departure. The US Antiterrorism Act 2002 (HR 3983) authorizes American ports to refuse entry to suspect vessels and conduct security assessments in foreign ports. The governments of Hong Kong, Singapore and Malaysia are among those that have US customs inspectors stationed at their ports. The International Ship and Port-Facility Security (ISPS) code, a global initiative by the International Maritime Organization (IMO), requires the mandatory installation of a Ship Security Alert System for all new vessels above 500 GRT and the designation of on-board security officers for each of the approximately 50,000 vessels in the world merchant fleet. The core of the ISPS is the mandatory development and implementation of ship security plans, which must be approved either by flag states or delegated Recognized Security Organizations. Amendments to the 1974 International Convention for the Safety of Life at Sea (SOLAS) further require the embossing of registration numbers on the hulls of ships. Both initiatives were adopted by the IMO in December 2002 and came into effect from 1 July 2004. The IMO is also working to address the issue of port security through a Code of Practice on Security in Ports, adopted in December 2003. The ARF Statement on Cooperation against Piracy and Other Threats to Maritime Security, adopted in June 2003, included the warning—'The potential for terrorist attacks on vulnerable sea shipping threaten the growth of the Asia-Pacific region and the stability of global commerce' (ASEAN 2003). However, large ships such as tankers are difficult to sink or to manoeuvre, and hazardous cargo except liquefied petroleum gas (LPG) is usually carried in non-volatile form. Moreover, the organization and resources needed to mount major terrorist attacks at sea compared with the greater publicity generated by attacks on land have deterred most radical groups from attempting such operations (Graham 2006: 53–5).

PIRACY

The IMO definition of piracy derives from Article 101 of LOSC 1982: 'any illegal acts of violence or detention, or any act of depredation directed at private ships or aircraft on (or above) the high sea'. The IMB, reflecting its focus on preventing maritime crime, has adopted a more inclusive definition: 'any act of boarding or attempting to board any ship with the intent to commit theft or any other crime and with the intent or capability to use force in the furtherance of that act' (Abyankar 2001: 11). The IMO's 'high seas only' definition of piracy has been criticized as overly restrictive since the vast majority of illegal activities against ships (and aircraft) take place within territorial and archipelagic waters, and EEZs. The IMB's broader definition has also been criticized by some shipping associations as exaggerating the scale of the piracy problem by including acts of petty theft committed against ships in port. The differing definitions of the IMO and the IMB are said to have been harmonized when the IMO Assembly adopted its Code of Practice for the Investigation of Crimes of Piracy and Armed Robbery against Ships in November 2001. According to IMO Resolution A922(22), Article 2.2, 'Armed robbery against ships mean any unlawful act of violence or detention or any act of depredation, or threat thereof, other than an act of "piracy" directed against a ship or against persons or property on board such ship, within a State's jurisdiction over such offences'. It is believed that several piracy incidents go unreported by shipping companies, which tend to weigh the slim probability of recovering stolen property and apprehending pirates unfavourably against the risk of raised insurance premiums and the prohibitive cost of charter delays incurred during port-side investigations. The IMB has identified several types of modern piracy. First, there is the practice of illegally boarding vessels under way, at night and from the rear, for the purpose of theft. Second, there are robberies directed at easily removable property or valuables aboard ships at anchor. Third, there is 'military piracy' involving uniformed personnel in attacks on shipping for material gain. These uniformed personnel can belong to terrorist groups, in which case there is an overlap with terrorism-at-sea. There have also been allegations that some such incidents have had covert or tacit governmental/military involvement. Fourth, there are ship hijacks, beyond the range of coastal law enforcement, intended to appropriate and offload cargo to another vessel or at a friendly port. Such incidents can involve a high level of organization and violence. Joint coast guard patrols, international law enforcement cooperation, and activities targeted ashore have been suggested as measures to combat piracy. In any case, piracy is not considered to be a systemic threat to international shipping and trade in the way that military obstruction of SLOC or terrorism-at-sea causing mass destruction or economic damage can be (Graham 2006: 55–8).

Coming back to SLOC in general, the military aspect in regional contexts continues to be important. Grove (1993: 169–70) has noted that the deployment of ultra-quiet, conventionally-powered attack submarines (known in short as SSKs after the hull classification symbol used by the US Navy) may become an important equalizer, helping smaller, poorer countries defend themselves from richer, stronger assailants. In the event of regional maritime tensions, if strong regional powers acquire submarine forces and develop doctrine to employ them against SLOC (which also happen to be major shipping routes), there could be systemic consequences for international shipping and trade (Graham 2006: 59–60).

According to Graham (2006: 61–2), there is widespread consensus that chokepoints are the most vulnerable segments of SLOC and concerns that regional conflicts could interrupt international shipping flows reflect the proximity of regional 'flash-points' to chokepoint straits where merchant shipping is concentrated. Most such waterways, if used in transit, could probably be bypassed at an acceptable economic cost. However, the scope for diversion narrows as ships approach their terminals; the concentration of container traffic, particularly around numerous hub-ports, augments this aspect of SLOC vulnerability. He argues that while in 'total war' the distinction between 'military' and 'economic' SLOC may break down, such a distinction could be useful since contemporary SLOC threats are likely to arise below the threshold of total war. Here, the term 'military SLOC' applies when SLOC are used to project military power, while 'economic SLOC' applies for conduct of trade.

CONCLUSION

Thinking about ocean space in terms of military strategy largely involves thinking about 'using' it by actual or threatened force, in the interest of one country or group of countries, against the interest of another country or group of countries. The LOSC 1982 can be thought of as an attempt to provide a set of rules aimed at peacefully 'regulating the use' of ocean space in the interest of all countries. The stronger the link between a country's national economy and the international or regional economy, the greater will be the importance of 'economic SLOC' to it.

However, one needs to qualify this by pointing out that below the threshold of 'total war' a country is unlikely to exhaust its stockpiles of necessary materials to sustain a war effort. Therefore, even if a country's economy is closely linked to the international or regional, below the threshold of 'total war' 'economic SLOC' may not be of crucial importance to its war effort, whereas in 'total war' they are certain to be of vital importance to the war effort. Given that ships facilitate about 90 per cent of international trade (Shipping Facts 2012), sea lanes are vital to the functioning of the international or regional economy. Military strategy prescribes 'convoys' (merchant ships escorted by naval ships) and 'patrolling' as ways in which a country can secure SLOC that are important to it. In a context of shared sea lanes, however, securing one's own SLOC can make those of another country insecure. The LOSC 1982 and other related institutional mechanisms for international cooperation seek to provide a system of regulations for making sea lanes secure for all countries. Military strategic prescriptions for securing SLOC/sea lanes such as convoys and patrolling should be subsumed within such a system of regulations in the form of joint multilateral operations. Alongside inter-state conflict, terrorism-at-sea and piracy have emerged as significant threats to the security of SLOC/sea lanes in recent years.

CHAPTER TWO

Maritime Cooperation in South Asia

South Asia's strategic architecture has undergone a major transition. Trends in economic development have produced new regional economic/military powers, providing the resources for extensive defence modernization and fundamentally altering the character of security concerns. New areas of potential conflict, such as disputes over competing sovereignty claims, repressed by the superpower rivalry and other Cold War dynamics, now demand consideration on a priority basis. The prospects for conflict and/or cooperation in the Indian Ocean are affected by many factors, and these prospects directly influence the security environment of the Indian Ocean littoral and island states of South Asia. Earlier attempts to improve the Indian Ocean security environment through the ideology of non-alignment, regional cooperation and adherence to the UN Charter have not been very successful. With the passage of time, the security environment can be expected to deteriorate, turning the area into a 'zone of conflict' rather than a 'zone of peace and cooperation'. According to a study of 175 armed conflicts between 1945 and the mid-1980s, Europe and North America were largely free of them as most of them taking place in Third World countries, mostly on the continents of Asia and Africa (Singh 1984: 1). However, the developed countries played a considerable indirect role in these armed conflicts, in the form of arms supplies, political moves or the use of force without active participation. The demise of the bipolar world has generated more factionalism and strife in Africa and Asia due to sub-nationalism, ethnic cleansing, religious extremism, famines, and environmental degradation. The South Asian littoral and island states of the Indian Ocean have been particularly vulnerable since most of them are brittle underdeveloped countries with little financial or industrial stamina to withstand the dictates of developed nations. The need for regional maritime cooperation in South Asia also merits serious attention in view of transnational threats such as narco-terrorism, sea piracy, smuggling, and illegal fishing. These peace-time operations include monitoring non-military threats; delineating maritime boundaries; preventing illegal migration; and scrutinizing the scramble for marine resources such as oil and fish. South Asian countries will need to increasingly turn to regional maritime powers for cooperation in marine affairs, and for support in ensuring the integrity of their respective EEZs (Alam 1997: 19–21).

The northern Indian Ocean just off South Asia contains important SLOC and maritime chokepoints. A large volume of international long-haul maritime cargo from the Persian Gulf, Africa and Europe transits via this area. This maritime trade, much of which is oil, is essential to the daily lives of many people around the world. The main shipping lane transiting the northern Indian Ocean and entering the strategic chokepoints of Southeast Asia has great strategic significance. Under these conditions, the northern Indian Ocean is bustling with maritime activity, involving both economic and security aspects. By its geographical location, the Indian subcontinent lies approximately halfway between the Strait of Hormuz in the west and the Strait of Malacca in the east. Both these chokepoints are major potential flashpoints. Although there are alternatives to the Strait of Malacca, there are no routes to transport the Persian Gulf oil other than through pipelines over land, which have their own vulnerabilities. Hence any contingency in the Strait of Hormuz has direct implications for the region. Geographically, the Indian peninsula dominates the SLOC from the Persian Gulf before they round off south of Dondra Head in southern Sri Lanka. Further, these SLOC pass close to the Indian Andaman and Nicobar Islands prior to entering the Strait of Malacca. Within this geopolitical setting, the security environment in the northern Indian Ocean faces numerous challenges. Some of them can potentially disrupt and destroy peaceful maritime enterprise. The region is plagued by piracy, drug smuggling, gunrunning, and illegal migration, which challenge order at sea and threaten peaceful use of the seas (Sakhuja 2001: 188, 198).

This chapter will examine prospects for maritime cooperation in South Asia to combat these threats in accordance with LOSC 1982, both within and outside SAARC's institutional framework. An effort has also been made to justify the fundamental rationale for South Asian maritime cooperation posited by this study—the emerging regionalization of the South Asian economy, which would entail a greater degree of attention to the issue of protection of sea lanes and merchant shipping in the years ahead. In looking at the prospects for such cooperation, outside of yet complementary to SAARC, it will seek to draw lessons from the Jakarta Centre for Law Enforcement Cooperation (JCLEC) established in the neighbouring Southeast Asian region.

TOWARDS A SAARC CENTRE FOR MARITIME COOPERATION

Bangladesh, Bhutan, India, The Maldives, Nepal, Pakistan, and Sri Lanka formed SAARC in December 1985 to improve the economies of more than one-fifth of the world's population that lives in South Asia. The SAARC Charter specifically excluded bilateral and contentious issues from its agenda. Nevertheless, SAARC has provided a unique opportunity for heads of government, ministers, and senior representatives of member states to regularly meet and exchange views on subjects of common concern. The leaders have used the opportunity to bilaterally discuss sensitive subjects like Kashmir, the South Asian nuclear issue, the Tamil question, and water disputes. In many cases, these discussions have helped manage and contain unstable situations, provided for constructive follow-up action, and even facilitated agreements. Functionally and pragmatically motivated interaction spurred by membership in SAARC has worked to decrease sources of tension. The process has been a gradual one, requiring the identification of areas of mutuality and 'binding together those interests which are common, where they are common, and to the extent to which they are common' (Khan 1991: 153–4). On occasion, when bilateral inter-state tensions were at a point at which bilateral processes of reconciliation were totally suspended, contacts initiated within the SAARC framework have continued to be effective, facilitating the process of crisis management. Such cooperation increases interaction at different levels, helps confidence building and creates new priorities of peace among nations. The SAARC Preferential Trading Arrangement (SAPTA) was incorporated into the SAARC framework in 1993 and came into force in December 1995. This was an effort to effect significant tariff cuts for imports within the region to increase intra-regional trade. Such meaningful cooperation at the regional and sub-regional levels can promote understanding and reconciliation among states, even leading to the resolution of long-standing problems (Alam 1997: 21–2). In 2004, at the 12th SAARC summit in Islamabad, the SAFTA agreement was concluded, and it came into force in January 2006. In April 2007, at SAARC's 14th summit, Afghanistan became its eighth member. SAARC has also granted 'observer status' to Australia, China, European Union (EU), Iran, Japan, Mauritius, Myanmar, South Korea and the US (SAARC 2012a, Table 1).

Mohd. Khurshed Alam (1997: 24–6) has argued that security in South Asia has a lot to do with maritime issues. Waterways through the region are strategically important for both merchant and naval vessels. Coastal and offshore resources provide principal means of livelihood in many countries of the region. For the island countries, external threats can only come over, on, or under sea. The realities of geopolitical and geostrategic imperatives point towards South Asia being a 'zone of conflict' rather than a 'zone of peace'. Its states can act both individually and collectively to build confidence in the region. Acting individually, self-reliance can only come about through internal strength and stability, economic development, and a naval strategy to provide effective and credible sea power to safeguard national interests. Throughout South Asia, security concerns have broadened to include economic and environmental issues. Economic security involves not only the protection of SLOC but also the protection of fish stocks and other marine resources. The LOSC 1982 introduced new uncertainties to the region, related to the EEZ, disputes over islands, continental

TABLE 1: PARTICIPANTS IN THE SAARC

	Members	Observers
	Afghanistan	Australia
	Bangladesh	China
	Bhutan	European Union
	India	Iran
	The Maldives	Japan
	Nepal	Mauritius
	Pakistan	Myanmar
	Sri Lanka	South Korea
	–	United States
	–	–
Total	**8**	**9**

Sources: Alam (1997: 21), SAARC (2012a).

shelf claims, and other offshore issues. Many emerging economic security concerns in the region such as oil, illegal fishing, and exploitation of other offshore resources are essentially maritime in nature. Fisheries are an important source of nutrition and protein yet many countries lack sufficient information and infrastructure relevant to sea fish resources and their exploitation and sustenance. Information about marine mineral resources in the region is limited as most of the ocean resources have not been adequately surveyed. In addition, the EEZ has generated requirements for naval capabilities for surveillance over resource-rich areas, which are for some states in the region almost equal to, or greater than, their land area. There are important maritime dimensions in military, economic, and environmental aspects of regional security. The requirements of monitoring SLOC and EEZs, coordinating weather prediction, and monitoring oil spills and other pollution demand greater maritime surveillance capabilities. The prevention of drug trafficking, disaster management, and other economic and environmental problems are also likely to require escort ships, offshore vessels, and maritime surveillance capabilities. For coastal South Asian countries, maritime demands have required a reorientation of planning and capabilities, away from the land theatre and towards the maritime theatre.

Alam (1997: 31–3) suggests that processes of confidence building and security enhancement in South Asia must necessarily be heavily weighted towards maritime mechanisms. Maritime concerns have been reflected in myriad confidence building proposals, which ought to have been the subject of serious discussion in the region. Ballistic missile capabilities are likely to generate offsetting acquisitions elsewhere and trigger an unanticipated, undesired arms race. It is therefore particularly necessary that these acquisitions are transparent and accompanied by dialogue. Many of the new maritime weapon systems, such as submarine warfare systems and long-range anti-ship missiles requiring over-the-horizon targeting, are potential sources of accidents and mandate measures to avoid incidents at sea. Concerns over piracy and illegal activities throughout many of the EEZs in the region can best be addressed through cooperative surveillance and/or information sharing arrangements. The region's diversity in terms of security interests, perceptions and military capabilities, presence of territorial disputes, insurgency, cultural/religious predispositions, and the experience in developing cooperative mechanisms/processes in other fields such as economic relations indicates that the process of maritime confidence building in South Asia will be slow and painstaking. An information exchange network could be a unique forum and a significant first step towards enhanced understanding between the region's navies and other maritime forces. The initial focus of such cooperative activities should be on operational matters, directed toward particular concerns, perhaps mostly non-military in nature, beginning with basic modes and procedures for information exchange rather than the erection of new institutional structures for multilateral maritime surveillance efforts. A list of concerns such as maritime pollution and environmental concerns, weather prediction, high sea robbery/piracy, fisheries infringements, SAR, suspicious activity indicating possible narcotics trafficking could be placed on the agenda. The development of common procedures for communication between the navies of the region and merchant vessels could provide a capability, the significance of which for regional confidence building will far transcend the particular purposes of any consulate. The process of consensus among naval authorities on the priority areas for information exchange will enhance regional appreciation of particular national concerns and interests as well as intensify understanding among navies. The operation of such a network could be assisted by the use of the region's navies. Naval headquarters at the national level are more or less competent managers of information, able to analyse information and propose action. A similar institutional centre at the regional level under SAARC may offer a useful starting point for an international network for surveillance, safety, and information exchange. For the community of navies in the region, it would also provide a framework to deal with possible situations at sea, should they ever arise. For the wider marine community, navy-to-navy links could be convenient paths to reach equivalent agencies in other countries. Cooperation on marine safety can cover SOLAS, navigational services, and prevention of shipping accidents. Marine safety is implemented through a system of Port State Control (PSC), which includes efficient inspection when ships are at port, maintenance of data on sub-standard ships, and exchange of information among participating countries. Although the PSC system is prevalent in other regions, no efforts were made to introduce such a system in South Asia as of the late 1990s.[1] Maritime safety and anti-pollution measures have not been effective in the area either. SAR systems for rescue of survivors, ship reporting, safety communications, and satellite-aided tracking systems must also be developed in the region. Regional cooperation could also include marine environmental protection, marine science, and technology and oceanography.

Navies have traditionally assumed the role of protecting SLOC along with other maritime forces. A case can also be made generally for navy-to-navy cooperation in areas such as information exchange, high-seas patrol in the suppression of violence at sea from criminal/terrorist activity, and illegal cross-

[1] However, an Indian Ocean Memorandum of Understanding on PSC, with a secretariat in Goa, India, came into effect on 1 April 1999. By August 2011, India, The Maldives, Sri Lanka and Bangladesh were among the 16 countries that had become party to it (IOMOU 2012).

border flow of drugs and economic/political refugees. Navies have always had independent roles in policing the high seas, beyond the jurisdiction of coastal states, in pursuit of pirates, slavers, and mutineers. With increasing interdependence of economies and the diminished responsibility of countries of registry, the navy's role of high seas patrol and surveillance and subsequent information management should be extended to other examples of criminal activity such as negligence and incompetence. All navies share a number of duties of surveillance and enforcement on the high seas. These duties could be carried out with much closer cooperation in terms of information sharing. In practical terms for ships at sea, this extension of a navy's charter could be achieved in many unthreatening ways in all sea regimes, including during innocent passage, as extensions of the mariners' customary duties and obligations. These could include a policy of regular environmental sampling, periodically surveying areas in dispute; the development of expertise in pollution counter-measures/weather prediction, enabling ships to provide 'first aid' in environmental disasters; reporting of substandard bridgemanship, particularly in cases of flagrant breaches of the International Regulations for Preventing Collisions at Sea; assistance to shore authorities in identifying rogue shipping in areas of cooperation; and a willingness to share significant information with all sea users. In this case, a general understanding on entry into territorial seas of other parties unintentionally or through force majeure, a uniform interpretation of the rules of innocent passage, agreement on restriction of certain maritime areas to particular operations, agreement on minimum distances of approach between naval ships, and provision for uninterrupted communication to avert or peacefully resolve any incidents, should be arrived at by the region's navies.

To facilitate such a process, Alam (1997: 33–4) has called for the formation of an institutional structure within SAARC for a CMC encompassing the full range of maritime affairs. Such a structure would provide opportunity to establish common interests, propose solutions, and consolidate action. The maritime community tends to be more internationalist, less concerned with issues of national prestige, than its land counterpart, partly because they share a common enemy—the sea itself—and partly because a lot of their operating area is international by nature. The twenty-first century is expected to witness a large increase in international trade and hence seaborne trade as well. There is an increasing need for peace and security in South Asia and for the region to be insulated from external pressure. North–South arms transfers have threatened to destabilize the international system. In such a position of great uncertainty, navies have represented a force of stability. Moreover, economic factors can force the major naval powers of the region to cooperate. Considering the need of the hour, the urgency to deal with maritime issues and to initiate the process of confidence building among military players in the region, it was suggested that Bangladesh table a proposal within SAARC for setting up a CMC. It was felt that such a proposal would best progress if it were relatively modest and informal, did not depend on new institutional structures, did not impinge on core national interests and defence capabilities, and addressed lower-profile security issues such as piracy, SAR, drug trafficking, terrorism, offshore pollution control, SLOC management, and weather prediction. It was expected to provide for more structured regional confidence building and security enhancement, the institutionalization of a regional dialogue on maritime issues being one of the most fundamental building blocks. Such a dialogue could lead to better appreciation of concerns, interests, and perceptions of participating countries; enhance mutual understanding and trust; and prevent misinterpretations, misunderstandings, and suspicions likely to cause conflict. The suggested objectives of such a CMC were as follows:

1. To foster maritime cooperation and dialogue among the SAARC states and to promote maritime confidence and security building measures;
2. To promote adherence to the principles of the LOSC 1982, to commence dialogue on the areas of LOSC 1982 which are either indefinite or not fully accepted by regional nations, and to promote joint hydrographic survey efforts to assist in the observance and implementation of LOSC 1982;

3. To help safeguard the peaceful merchant shipping of the region and to examine the means for developing procedures to assist in the protection of shipping within the region with increased joint activity in naval control of shipping;
4. to create a secure atmosphere for the sustained exploitation of the resources of the sea and to identify regional hydrographic survey and oceanographic priorities and examine ways to conduct joint surveys in those waters with greatest priority;
5. to contribute to the preservation of the marine environment and to provide a framework of cooperation for weather prediction; and
6. to undertake policy-oriented studies on specific regional maritime security problems and to provide training in relevant aspects of maritime operations to those lacking in certain types of capability or expertise.

Alam (1997: 37–9) has argued that the fraternity of the sea transcends barriers of race, religion, language, and nationality. Navies of the region could be considered as messengers of friendship and goodwill, and are often used as the handmaidens of peaceful diplomacy. Regional cooperation must take centrestage in the emerging maritime order. Navies will need to transform the psychology of 'preparing for war to ensure peace' into 'if you want peace, prepare to cooperate'. Naval cooperation could be a way towards a more cost-effective use of scarce and expensive naval resources such as training facilities for basic/advanced engineering skills, electrical and electronic skills, submarine training tactical work-up, and other infrastructure facilities. A wide range of opportunities for navy-to-navy cooperation could be placed on the agenda of a SAARC CMC. These may include joint schemes for ocean surveillance, transparency in procurement, combined operational exercises, joint procedure for relief of natural disasters and weather prediction, pooling of expertise in marine salvage, SAR, exchange of military personnel, and joint action in the enforcement of international law and order at sea. To cost effectively utilize the infrastructure of navies for national development as opposed to coercion and military functions, it might be better for countries to have common ship-plots and communication facilities for tasks such as quick response and rescue coordination. Naval cooperation could also take place in implementing the SOLAS promulgated by the IMO, monitoring nuclear waste disposal, preventing poaching and over-fishing, and deterring unauthorized population movements. The coast guard, where available, would be a vital adjunct of a SAARC CMC. However, despite Alam's convincing argument, no action seems to have been taken on this front till date.

RELATED DEVELOPMENTS

Nevertheless, many related developments are worth mentioning. According to internal documents of the Sri Lankan Police's Criminal Investigation Department (CID *c.* 1992, 2001), made available to the author, at the SAARC Meeting of Experts to Advance Cooperation under the SAARC Regional Convention on Suppression of Terrorism held at Colombo from 3 to 5 August 1992, Sri Lanka had proposed the setting up of a SAARC Terrorist Offences Monitoring Desk (STOMD) to exchange information in combating terrorism in the SAARC region. This unit was to be modelled along the lines of the SAARC Drug Offences Monitoring Desk (SDOMD), established in 1992 and located in the Sri Lanka Police's Narcotics Bureau. The setting up of the STOMD was meant to help the work of liaison officers appointed in each SAARC country to advance cooperation under the convention. The SAARC Council of Ministers, at its 12th session held at Dhaka in December 1992, approved the proposal for the establishment of STOMD. Accordingly, the STOMD has been in operation since 1995. A circular containing instructions pertaining to the exchange of information to combat terrorism together with an Initial Reporting (IR) Form and a Detailed Reporting (DR) Form was circulated to member states to maintain a database. However, the response from member states was negligible and therefore the STOMD was not able to achieve the desired objectives. During the Interpol General Assembly held at Seoul in November 1999, Dr R.K. Raghavan, Head of Interpol in India and Director of the Central Bureau of Investigation of India, initiated an ad hoc meeting with Interpol heads of SAARC countries to reactivate the STOMD. SAARC heads of delegations appreciated the initiative and attended this meeting, where Punya De Silva, head of the Sri Lankan delegation, agreed to host the next meeting in 2000 to discuss ways and means to reactivate the STOMD. However, this meeting could not be arranged due to unforeseen reasons.

After the 4th SAARC Annual Meeting of Liaison Officers for Exchange of Information on Suppression of Terrorism in Male in September 1997, the group could not convene till 2001. In December 2001, it was suggested that since all SAARC countries (expect Bhutan) would attend the 17th Interpol Asian Regional Conference in Sri Lanka in February 2002, a special meeting should be arranged for them to discuss the reactivation of the STOMD and to fix a date and venue for their 5th annual meeting. This proposal also suggested that the 11th SAARC Summit in Nepal would be an opportune moment to discuss the resurrection of the STOMD's activities. Workshops held at New Delhi on 23 and 24 February 2007 discussed, at length, matters relating to strengthening of the SDOMD and the STOMD, and made relevant recommendations. A meeting of national focal points of these two bodies was held on 20 October 2007 in Islamabad. At the third meeting of the national focal points of SDOMD, held on 23 June 2010 in Islamabad, Pakistan offered to strengthen the body by making a one-time financial/material assistance and to prepare a concept paper on interaction between SAARC and the United Nations Office on Drugs and Crime (UNODC) to be considered by all member states. Further, the governments of Bangladesh, Pakistan, and Sri Lanka offered training courses/programmes in fields related to narcotics and drugs. Realizing the importance of learning from each other's experiences, the member states agreed to submit country reports on the drug situations in their respective countries to the SDOMD and also to share information on a real-time, or near real-time, basis. At the third meeting of the STOMD, held on 23 June 2010 in Islamabad, member states decided to share information on a real-time basis and exchange data on many related areas such as terrorists, photographs, profiles, and incidents.

Action to be taken to improve/secure data exchanged through the networking among police authorities was also discussed at length (SAARC 2010a; 2010b).

The establishment of a regional CZMC was recommended in the 1992 SAARC study titled 'Causes and Consequences of Natural Disasters and the Protection and Preservation of the Environment'. Subsequently, the SCZMC was set-up and inaugurated in The Maldives in June 2005 (SCZMC 2011a; 2011b). The SCZMC seeks to promote cooperation in planning, management, and sustainable development of coastal zones, including research, training, and awareness generation in the region. Its terms of reference are as follows:

1. Identify the organizations in the region dealing with the relevant coastal resources management issues and facilitate interaction amongst institutions (ministries, coastal authorities, intergovernmental organizations, international organizations, NGOs, funding agencies) and other stakeholders involved, and promote coordination and cooperation on ICZM issues;
2. Collect, compile, and disseminate information through networking among the member states;
3. Assess and standardize the planning methodologies for ICZM;
4. Provide support for the promotion and development of ICZM concepts, methodologies, and planning tools;
5. Promote exchange of experiences, information, data, and expertise in ICZM;
6. Assist in institutional strengthening and human resources development for capacity building in ICZM and conduct and coordinate research in the field of CZM and facilitate technology transfer (SCZMC 2011c).

An expert group meeting held at Male on 25–6 April 2007 produced a SAARC Coastal Zone Management Action Plan (Appendix). All member states except Afghanistan and Nepal participated in the meeting. The draft action plan was submitted to the 4th Meeting of the Governing Board of the SCZMC for approval. It was approved by SAARC's 31st Programming

Committee and 34th Standing Committee held in December 2007.

In February 2011, speaking at the 33rd session of the SAARC Council of Ministers, Prof. G.L. Peiris, Sri Lanka's Minister of External Affairs, welcomed the proposal by The Maldives to develop principles of modern law relating to maritime security and piracy (*Daily News* 2011a). In an interview in April 2011, the author was informed by Azizuddin Ahmadzada and Ghulam Dastgir of the SAARC Secretariat that The Maldives was in the process of preparing a concept paper, which would be circulated to all the member country governments (Ahmadzada and Dastgir 2011).

COOPERATION OUTSIDE SAARC

With regard to cooperation outside SAARC, which can be complementary to it, valuable lessons can be learnt from the JCLEC established in the neighbouring Southeast Asian region. The JCLEC is situated within the Indonesian National Police Academy in Semarang, Indonesia. Its establishment was announced in February 2004 by the Indonesian and Australian governments, with Australia committing 36.8 million Australian dollars to support its development and operations through 2009. This initiative reflects the shared priority given to bilateral and regional cooperation on a variety of contemporary security issues. Since the announcement of the establishment of the centre, various countries have evinced interest in supporting its training role through the provision of technical assistance and funding. The centre is intended as a resource for Southeast Asia in the fight against transnational crime, with a focus on counter-terrorism. It will coordinate and facilitate a range of training programmes and thus assist governments in meeting their security interests and objectives in Southeast Asia. It will also be capable of responding to requests from regional governments for operational support in dealing with terrorism and other transnational crimes. Although conceived as a bilateral initiative, both Indonesia and Australia welcome participation by regional countries and contributions from the wider international community supportive of the centre's goals. The centre will work particularly closely with law enforcement agencies in Southeast Asia and cooperate, where possible, with existing centres such as the South East Asian Regional Centre for Counter Terrorism (SEARCCT) in Kuala Lumpur and the International Law Enforcement Academy in Bangkok. It will participate in work undertaken by the ad hoc working groups on law enforcement and legal issues established at the Bali Ministerial Meeting on Counter-Terrorism in February 2004 and related follow-up activities. This facility is expected to strengthen the capacity of foreign governments and law enforcement personnel to develop and attain complex security objectives in Southeast Asia (JCLEC 2011).

CONCLUSION

Alam (1997: 39–40) has noted that, while the setting up of a SAARC CMC may be a necessary goal, political tensions in the region have impaired progress. He suggests, as a first step towards setting up such a centre, the drafting of a regional framework for CBMs. These could include agreements on non-interference in naval manoeuvres, prevention of incidents at sea, and modalities for dealing with fishermen who stray into another nation's EEZ. A CMC would satisfy many important requirements in the region, address some very real issues, and serve as a building block in a more comprehensive maritime organization. That is to say, the process should begin modestly. Structured maritime surveillance systems may be feasible in particular circumstances where the commonality of interests is high or in situations where issues can best be addressed multilaterally. Multilateral maritime surveillance systems may be considered for challenges such as piracy control, weather prediction, and oil spill detection. The navies, coast guards, and police forces of the region can compile and share information on areas where piracy is most rampant, establish communication links, coordinate anti-piracy patrols, and organize joint sweeps against pirate strongholds. The establishment of specific-purpose multilateral surveillance systems in areas of particular concern and the strengthening of various bilateral maritime surveillance arrangements will help greatly in addressing the requirements of a CMC. Once a common reporting of formats and operating procedures have been developed, further initiatives with coordinated patrol and real-time information exchange may follow. Such a network, and the operational advantages it would confer, would be of great use in responding to other contingencies apart from the problems of piracy and pollution, such as the guidance and protection of peaceful shipping in the event of conflict and/or terrorism across SLOC in the region. While this would not be the initial purpose of the arrangement, it would be well within its capabilities. A comprehensive system of communication between navies would serve as a CBM, and contribute to the protection and restoration of peaceful shipping, the sustainable development and exploitation of sea resources, and the maintenance of the marine environment. It would also boost cooperation in the more traditional roles of navies in higher order conflicts. Initiatives for improving safety and security at sea involving only some of the countries in the region could be regionalized to the economic benefit of all countries. Alam has argued that seaborne trade could propel countries towards peace, and that peace and security in the region would, in turn, allow for greater seaborne trade, creating a mutually reinforcing dynamic that will directly contribute to the economic well-being of each country. However, as already noted, no action seems to have been taken till date regarding Alam's proposal. Nevertheless, some related developments have occurred in setting up the SDOMD and the STOMD and the ongoing efforts to strengthen them; setting up the SCZMC; and drafting the Maldivian proposal to develop principles of modern law relating to maritime security and piracy. Moreover, with regard to South Asian maritime cooperation outside SAARC which could at the same time be complementary to it, an important template can be derived from the establishment of the JCLEC in the neighbouring Southeast Asian region. While the JCLEC has been set up independently of ASEAN, it works closely with ASEAN-related bodies, which is something a body for South Asian maritime cooperation set up independently of SAARC can emulate. Such a body, while set up independently, could work closely with SAARC too.

When thinking about multilateral maritime cooperation in South Asia, two points are notable. First, let us consider Roy-Chaudhury's (1998: 275) argument, in the context of naval cooperation in the eastern sub-region of the Indian Ocean, that '. . . the development and growth of a web of bilateral naval relationships could, over a period of time, be made to evolve into a loosely defined multilateral set of activities. . . .' In South Asia, there has been considerable effort at maritime cooperation between India and Pakistan, as well as between India and Sri Lanka, particularly in the last few years, and both these bilateral cooperative relationships are ongoing.[2] If one goes by Roy-Chaudhury's argument, such bilateral maritime cooperation among South Asian countries could evolve into a 'loosely defined multilateral set of activities' with India playing a central and leading role. Second, it is important to locate South Asia as a continental sub-region within the Indian Ocean maritime region.[3] Just to illustrate, let us take Lehr's (2005: 11–13) suggestion that, multilateral security cooperation in the Indian Ocean should focus on the northern part of the Indian Ocean, consisting of the Bay of Bengal and the Arabian Sea. The Bay of Bengal is a sub-region of the Indian Ocean maritime region to the east of South Asia, and the Arabian Sea is a sub-region of the Indian Ocean maritime region to the west of South Asia. The Arabian Sea is situated between the continental sub-regions of South Asia and

[2] For India–Pakistan maritime cooperation, see Siddiqa-Agha (2000), Ansari & Vohra (2003), and Ghosh (2008). It is worth noting that Siddiqa-Agha's work formed the basis for the first symposium on 'Confidence and Cooperation in South Asian Waters' held in January 2001. That theme is an ongoing project of the Centre for Foreign Policy Studies (CFPS), Dalhousie University, and the eighth symposium was held in June 2011 (for further details, CFPS 2012). For India–Sri Lanka maritime cooperation, see Raju & Keethaponcalan (2006) and Vohra & Srivatsan (2008). These sources will be examined in greater detail in Chapter 3.

[3] This distinction between the continental region and the maritime region is taken from Singh (2004: 195).

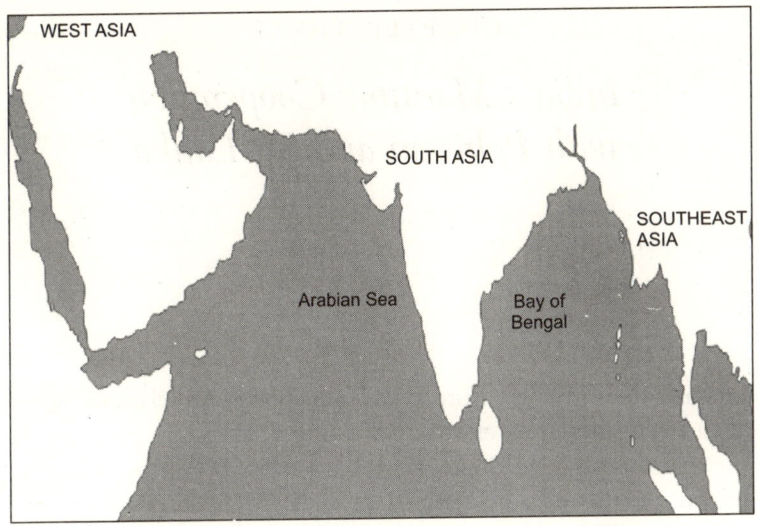

Source: Adapted from d-maps.com (2012).

MAP 1: LOCATING SOUTH ASIA AS A CONTINENTAL SUB-REGION WITHIN THE INDIAN OCEAN MARITIME REGION

West Asia (or the Middle East). The Bay of Bengal is situated between the continental sub-regions of South Asia and Southeast Asia (Map 1). If one thinks in these terms, multilateral maritime cooperation in South Asia may well overlap with multilateral maritime cooperation in West Asia (or the Middle East) and in Southeast Asia. In institutional terms, this translates into the reality that South Asian maritime cooperation within or outside SAARC may well have to be coordinated with maritime cooperation within the Gulf Cooperation Council (GCC) as well as within ASEAN. Therefore, while not much importance has been given to maritime cooperation *per se* within SAARC until recently, ongoing India–Pakistan and India–Sri Lanka bilateral cooperation efforts could evolve into South Asian multilateral cooperation within or outside SAARC. If and when it does, it may have to coordinate with maritime cooperation within the GCC and the ASEAN.

CHAPTER THREE

India's Maritime Cooperation with Pakistan and Sri Lanka

Despite the troubled history of India–Pakistan relations, there have been numerous efforts at building bilateral cooperation. In the maritime sphere, these efforts have taken the form of CBMs, which can be broadly defined as tools to reduce tension and avert war. This idea developed from the East–West experience of confidence building to minimize the threat of an accidental outbreak of conflict and war during the Cold War. The 1975 Helsinki Final Act and the 1990 Vienna Document are some of the agreements that formalized the means to reduce tension by exchanging information, developing communication channels, and adopting constraint measures to bolster confidence in each other's intentions. The primary idea was to introduce an element of predictability in the behaviour of hostile states so that tension would not escalate to an uncontrollable degree (Siddiqa-Agha 2000: 12). Efforts at India–Pakistan maritime cooperation go as far back as 1975, when they signed a protocol to the 1972 Simla Agreement titled 'Protocol on Resumption of Shipping Services between India and Pakistan'. More recently, however, Ansari and Vohra (2003: 24) and Ghosh (2008: 37) have called for its amendment, criticizing it as too restrictive.

India–Sri Lanka relations, which went through turbulence in the 1980s, have looked up since the 1990s and enjoy a very healthy status today. India–Sri Lanka maritime cooperation can be traced back to 1971 when, during the first Janatha Vimukthi Peramuna (JVP) insurrection, the then Sri Lankan Prime Minister Sirimavo Bandaranaike approached many countries, including India, for military assistance, and India responded by, among other measures, sending five frigates to seal off approaches to Colombo. Indian frigates helped in the surveillance of the coast to prevent the JVP receiving supplies through the sea. All Indian forces sent to Sri Lanka at the time were withdrawn by end-June 1971 (Suryanarayan 2008: 47).

International relations literature tends to consider bilateral and multilateral relations as two distinct spheres of activity, ignoring the fact that often bilateral conflict can stand in the way of multilateral cooperation. One of the best examples of this tendency comes from South Asia, where the troubled India–Pakistan bilateral relationship has been a major factor inhibiting South Asian multilateral cooperation. To get around this obstacle, this chapter attempts a bottom-up approach of building multilateral cooperation based on bilateral cooperation. It examines efforts at India–Pakistan and India–Sri Lanka maritime cooperation to identify common areas of cooperation, which could possibly be used as bases to evolve a contemporary agenda for South Asian maritime cooperation. However, prior to that, given the centrality of India to this structure of cooperation, it briefly discusses the 'India factor' in South Asian security.

THE 'INDIA FACTOR' IN SOUTH ASIAN SECURITY

Geographically, India is the fulcrum around which the region of South Asia revolves, situated as it is at the centre with the other countries arranged around it. India shares a land or maritime border with all the other South Asian countries except Afghanistan, while none of the other countries, except Afghanistan–Pakistan and Sri Lanka–The Maldives, share a border with each other. Nambiar (2009: 17) argues that in undertaking a security perspective of the South Asian region, India's sheer size (in terms of land mass, population, and resources) has to be kept in mind. Moreover, only India has shared ethnic affinities with sections of the population of each of its neighbours, except for some shared ethnicity between Nepal and Bhutan. Nambiar goes on to argue that an appreciation of this unique feature is important for an understanding of the complex inter-state political and security dynamics of the region because while there is a bilateral security dimension between each of the other South Asian countries and India, they have very little of the same with each other. He is of the view that if this is perceived as the price India has to pay for its geography and cultural history, it can also be viewed as a reasonable basis for evolving a cooperative security framework for South Asia.

It goes without saying that India has an unavoidable and crucial stake in the happenings in its immediate neighbourhood in South Asia. Instability and social upheaval in these countries will have inevitable and detrimental spillover effects on India, causing security problems and generating stress. Today, most major countries like the US, EU, Russia, and Japan would like to see India play a more proactive role in promoting democratic values and contributing to regional stability, as much because of their perception that India has the capability to do so as because they themselves do not wish to be physically involved. Perhaps the only limiting element here is India's inability to build national consensus on this and the consequent lack of political will. While there is little doubt that India has to take into account the sensitivities of its neighbours in deciding its approach to regional security, it would also be prepared to use its economic and military clout in the pursuit of such security. The fact that India straddles the Indian Ocean, imposes on it the responsibility to ensure the security of the sea lanes from the Persian Gulf to the Malacca Straits. In recent years, this has been acknowledged by some major international players. India's spontaneous and effective response to the Indian Ocean tsunami disaster of 2004 and recent naval action against pirates in the Gulf of Aden has reinforced this position. India's maritime capability should, therefore, be geared to meet this challenge. The diplomatic challenge is to initiate coordination with other countries of the Indian Ocean littoral (Nambiar 2009: 21). In this task, India will have to take cognizance of and actively seek to dispel concerns about 'Indian hegemony' in other South Asian countries (for example, Khan 2011).

INDIA–PAKISTAN MARITIME COOPERATION

Siddiqa-Agha's (2000) work formed the basis for the first symposium on 'Confidence and Cooperation in South Asian Waters', an ongoing project of the Centre for Foreign Policy Studies (CFPS) of Dalhousie University, Halifax, Canada. Eight symposiums have been held since as part of the project, the last one in June 2011. Issues discussed at these symposiums included prevention of incidents at sea (INCSEA); Sir Creek, maritime boundary, and continental shelf issues; the plight of detained fishermen; the law of armed conflict and rules of engagement (ROE) at sea; maritime emergency management including the development of a SAR initiative and maritime environmental protection; maritime trade; anti-piracy efforts; and the safety and security of offshore oil activity in the Arabian Sea. Given the involvement of retired senior naval officers of India and Pakistan in this project, it can be seen as a Track II forum on maritime cooperation. As Siddiqa-Agha (2000: 26) points out, the retired officers would have the liberty and the relevant experience of discussing matters of mutual maritime concern. The debates held during Track II workshops would have the dual benefit of paving the way for Track I contact between serving officials, and allow the two governments to consider options with greater freedom than they can at the Track I level.

According to Ansari and Vohra (2003), the areas for maritime confidence building in India–Pakistan relations are (1) territorial issues; (2) maritime trade; (3) fishing and fishermen's plight; and (4) naval and coastal force interactions.

1. Territorial Issues

(a) Maritime Boundary

The India–Pakistan maritime boundary is still undemarcated due to a dispute over Sir Creek (Map 2), an area in the deltaic region of the Indus River. It has been proposed that the two governments consider the following recommendations to delineate the maritime boundary.

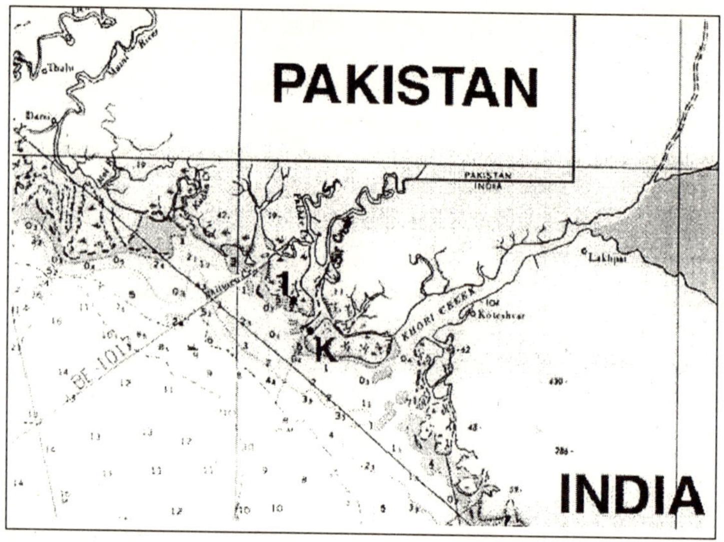

Notes: 1: Terminus of the Indian claim of the boundary line along the Western bank.

K: Terminus of the Pakistani claim of the boundary line along the Eastern bank.

Source: Ansari & Vohra (2003: 20).

MAP 2: SIR CREEK

1. Delink the Sir Creek dispute from the maritime boundary issue.
2. Agree to adopt the seaward approach in conformity with the UN document 'Technical Aspects of the Law of the Sea' up to a mutually agreed point from the coastline. The residual area from this point to the coast could be delineated at a later date pursuant to agreements regarding Sir Creek.

(b) Sir Creek

The Sir Creek dispute is documented to have originated in 1875 between the two princely states of Sind (now in Pakistan) and Kutch (now in India). In mid-1965, the Rann of Kutch area to the east of the Creek erupted in violent clashes, causing war between the two countries. After the war, the two sides referred the dispute to an arbitration panel, which published its decision on 19 February 1968, defining a new boundary between Kutch and Sind. At the panel's directive, the two sides were to erect pillars along the newly-defined boundary, but this task was not undertaken with any enthusiasm by either side. Thus, the demarcation of the boundary remains incomplete. Ansari and Vohra (2003) recommend that the most pragmatic solution to the dispute would be to let the boundary line fall in the middle of Sir Creek in accordance with the median/equidistant principle of international law. Till such a solution is mutually agreed upon, CBMs involving Sir Creek could advance relations and management of the area overall. LOSC 1982 has a provision for creation of maritime sensitive zones under mutual agreement. Such zones and areas, under interim arrangement, could either be jointly exploited or studied for environmental monitoring and ecological preservation, without prejudice to larger maritime claims of either side.

A joint study of this complex inter-tidal ecosystem, in accordance with LOSC 1982, may prove very useful. The study could either be focused on the Sir Creek area or be a larger project involving part of or the entire Karachi–Mumbai coastline. A sub-regional mechanism for cooperation under LOSC 1982 also exists as the South Asian Seas Action Plan (SASAP). The Indian and Pakistani governments have agreed to this regional plan along with the governments of other cooperating South Asian countries. A key element of SASAP is to encourage collaboration among regional scientists and technicians and their institutions to study various processes occurring in the coastal areas and open ocean, as well as sources/levels of pollutants and their effects on marine life and human health. SASAP provides India and Pakistan with a framework for sharing environmental release and effluent data in the Sir Creek and coastal regions. A joint project may promote understanding of ecological and physical aspects of Sir Creek as also alleviate tensions in the area of dispute.

2. Maritime Trade

(a) Shipping and Trade

Pursuant to the Simla Agreement in 1972, both countries signed the 1974 Protocol on Resumption of Trade, followed in January 1975 by the Protocol on Resumption of Shipping Services.

However, the clauses of the 1975 Protocol were so restrictive on ship registrations, cargo volumes, equality principles and so on that it actually resulted in a sharp decline in trade. Though it was to be reviewed yearly, the protocol did not come up for review until 1984. The Shipping Protocol stipulates: 'Neither country can lift third country liner cargo originating from the ports of either country and destined for ports in third countries and vice versa.' Indian ships are not allowed to carry cargo from Pakistan to any country other than India, nor can Pakistani ships carry cargo from Indian ports to any third country. This has worked to the detriment of shipping concerns on both sides of the border by restricting them to bilateral cargo, which is insignificant. It has also been pointed out by Ansari and Vohra (2003) that official India–Pakistan trade figures are misleading as they do not reflect the annual clandestine transactions of over 3 billion dollars conducted largely through unofficial monetary channels of *hundi* and *havala* (informal banking systems where transactions are covered by a chit system or simply word of mouth). Payments are made and accepted in either country, either by direct communication or via agents in Singapore, Dubai, or other Persian Gulf ports. Bilateral trade in 1948–9 was between 35–50 per cent of the two countries' total trade but has since dwindled to 1 per cent or lower, because of restrictive tariff barriers. Pakistan has a list of 600 items that may be imported from India, but the high import duties make them non-competitive, thus encouraging smuggling and indirect trade via third countries. These trade practices have served Pakistani consumers badly, while reaping huge profits for a nexus of shady businessmen, corrupt politicians, officials, smugglers, and criminals. The UN *Human Development Report 2002* estimated that open trading with India would reduce the cost of foodstuffs in Pakistan by 20–30 per cent. To allow unrestricted flow of trade, it is necessary to revise the Shipping Protocol of 1975. There is a mechanism whereby the India–Pakistan Joint Commission can be convened to remove the restrictive clauses 5 and 9 of the protocol, thus freeing up movement of goods and cargo in ships owned, operated, and chartered by either country. This would result in manifold increases of direct trade and reduction in shipping time and freight charges. It would discourage smuggling and bring profits to national carriers. This CBM is not highly sensitive politically and is unlikely to cause any repercussions, since it is beneficial to both countries. It is not inconceivable that ship owners may enter into joint ventures to maximize profits. Considering the restoration of passenger services between Karachi and Mumbai as a CBM has also been recommended.

(b) Security of Ports and Cargo

Following the 9/11 terrorist attacks in the US, the security of ports, their vulnerability to violence and disaster, and the resilience of a port complex have become urgent concerns. The emerging threat of smuggling radioactive materials and the endemic issues of smuggling drugs and contraband items are driving port authorities to improve security measures. However, the security problem is complicated by the nature of the maritime shipping business and the physical location of most ports. Many of them are wide open and easily accessible from both land and water. They are surrounded by large population centres, congested with multiple agencies operating around the clock. The ports are saddled with intensely competitive cargo handling regimes, obsolete transaction practices, institutional corruption, and poor communications. All these factors combine to raise serious security concerns. Popular perception does not associate ports with terrorism but the fact is that flags of convenience and registrations represent the soft underbelly of the maritime world. Some of these concerns place the free flow of trade, and thus freedom of navigation, firmly on the contemporary international agenda. Ports and transportation measures need to be developed and harmonized both regionally and globally. Unilateral efforts to tighten security within one country without commensurate efforts in neighbouring countries would remain ineffectual. The global economy and trade have to be protected. It is critical for maritime nations to strike a balance between security and free movement of trade.

In the context of India and Pakistan, adequate port and cargo security measures would help foster confidence prior to restoration of unrestricted shipping and trade. Effective security measures warrant a layered defence approach and transparency of goods and personnel movement. Crew identification, container tagging and tracking, communication, and database technologies can promote transparency via information sharing between port authorities of Karachi, Port Qasim, Mumbai, Kochi, and Chennai. The port authorities and partners participating in bilateral agreements would be in a position to monitor ships, container movements, and flow of goods and to develop robust risk management practices. As confidence grows, data and information on security measures can be shared. If Pakistani and Indian ports each enter into bilateral agreements with the US, in the context of US initiatives such as Operation Safe Commerce (OSC) and CSI, it would be expedient and logical to complete the triangle by entering into bilateral agreements locally. In this context, the following recommendations have been made to improve port and cargo security.

- Reform practices, streamline procedures, and upgrade facilities.
- Share data regarding crews and cargos.
- Share security information.
- Negotiate local bilateral agreements modelled after the US CSI.

3. Fishing and Fishermen's Plight

Fishermen have been fishing using traditional methods in the waters off the coasts of the Indian state of Gujarat and the Pakistani province of Sind for centuries, and they know all about the seasonal migratory trends of fish, which do not uphold any national boundary. Pakistani boats go over to Indian territory to catch pomfret, grouper, prawns, and shrimp while Indian boats go over to Pakistani waters in search of squid, ribbon fish, red snapper, and tiger prawn. In the process, some fishermen stray deep into the territory of the other country. In most cases, this happens due to lack of adequate instrumentation on-board the vessels, especially in smaller traditional boats that do not even carry radio sets. Most of these fishermen are poor and hired by wealthy contractors, who provide only the very basic amenities to the crew and tend to take minimal responsibility in case the fishermen transgress the international boundary and get arrested. Release of fishermen, who languish in jail for extended periods, and their boats, is announced from time to time by the leaders of the two countries as goodwill gestures. The issue of fishermen getting arrested by the law enforcement agency of another country is not unique to India and Pakistan. Numerous incidents of a similar nature take place in almost all coastal parts of the world. What is distressing is that whereas most other nations have resolved this issue by laying down certain rules through bilateral agreements, India and Pakistan have failed to address this essentially humanitarian issue.

The practice of fishermen crossing the international maritime boundary is unlikely to stop even after the boundary issue between India and Pakistan is resolved. Only operational cooperation and coordination and establishment of communications between the Indian Coast Guard (ICG) and Pakistan's Maritime Security Agency (MSA) ships at sea may help mitigate the suffering of fishermen and their families. With regard to this problem, the following recommendations have been made.

- Instructions can be issued by both governments not to arrest fishermen unless they are found indulging in illegal activities like narcotics trafficking and smuggling. It is understood that the prime ministers of both countries came to such an understanding at Lahore in February 1999. However, subsequent political events did not give the two governments sufficient time to implement the understanding. As part of this solution, the fishing area and the operational framework need to be defined and notified.
- Boats found in each other's territory could be warned and escorted back into their respective country's area. This would require continuous presence of patrol craft, for which both sides may not have enough resources.
- Both countries could grant fishing licences to a specified number of boats of the other country on a monthly/seasonal/yearly basis, limiting the total permissible quantity of catch on an annual basis.

A number of technical proposals have also been made, including the following:

- Creation of a 40 × 40 NM Zone of Disengagement (ZoD) straddling the disputed maritime boundary in which fishing boats from both India and Pakistan would be permitted to operate.
- Formation of a joint commission to oversee the ZoD.
- Involvement of local fishing community unions in the legal process, and encouragement to fishery unions of both countries to establish contact.
- Introduction of technologies such as transponders and vessel monitoring systems, which can be used by each country to warn vessels when they are crossing over into each other's territory (Encouraging fishermen to install such equipment on-board vessels would require cost subsidization. A database of fishing boats and crews could be maintained by each country, which would be useful in crew tagging, boat tracking, and identifying boats and crews in case of arrest. In time, the two databases could be linked and the fishermen's unions of both countries given access.)

4. Naval and Coastal Force Interactions

(a) INCSEA and Law of Naval Warfare

In April 1991, India and Pakistan concluded an agreement on advance notice of military exercises, manoeuvres, and troop movements. This agreement, though important from the military point of view, does not address issues of safety and security of smaller units, non-combatants, and neutral ships/aircraft. The need for a more comprehensive agreement to prevent incidents at sea was recognized by both India and Pakistan and incorporated in the Memorandum of Understanding (MoU) to the Lahore Declaration of February 1999. The Cooperative Monitoring Centre of Sandia National Laboratories, Albuquerque (New Mexico) and the CFPS, Dalhousie University, Halifax (Canada) in their publications and seminars have promoted and endorsed this clause as a significant CBM. Participants at the 2002 Symposium on Confidence Building in South Asian Waters, held at Kuala Lumpur, Malaysia, recognized the urgent need for an INCSEA-type agreement and recommended the Malaysia–Indonesia model as a suitable precedent. This agreement was preferred because it 'made creative and explicit provision for its application to the operation of their ships in disputed waters without prejudice to their respective claims' (CoMC 2002). INCSEA is not an end in itself but a beginning; it may not prevent all incidents but it will catalyse a change in relationship. In connection with INCSEA, it has been recommended that Indian and Pakistani navies consider a revision and update to their respective ROE to conform with the *San Remo Manual on International Law Applicable to Armed Conflicts at Sea*. If revised and implemented, customary law regulating armed conflict would become common law with regard to India and Pakistan. This would:

- codify ROE to be in conformity with international law;
- provide commonality of doctrine, which would produce predictable actions/reactions in areas of congruity;
- be recognized internationally as a set of rules to be used in courts, if needed; and
- create a common grid and range of mutual interests.

The adoption and promulgation of a common law of naval warfare by India and Pakistan would pave the way for the conclusion of INCSEA as a natural corollary.

(b) Indian Coast Guard (ICG)–Pakistani Maritime Security Agency (MSA) Cooperation

Both the ICG and the MSA are paramilitary forces operating under the defence ministries of their respective countries. These forces are not structured as fighting arms like the navies. The Charter of Duties assigned to both are similar; they are broadly responsible for the following activities in their respective areas.

- Protection of fishermen
- SAR at sea
- Assistance in disaster management at sea
- Anti-piracy exercises
- Anti-smuggling exercises
- Interdiction of narcotics trade and gun-running
- Protection of the marine environment
- Pollution control, especially from oil spills.

The listed activities can be executed effectively by ensuring certain synergy between the ICG and the MSA. This implies functional cooperation and coordination of operations at sea between the two services. To bring about the required level of understanding, the following incremental steps have been recommended:

1. A tabletop exercise involving at least one senior officer each from the ICG and the MSA on SAR, oil spill pollution control, or any other incident, should be conducted in a neutral country. The aim should be to promote understanding between the officers and evolve common procedures for operations at sea.
2. The next logical step would be to hold an actual joint exercise at sea.
3. Once this second step is achieved, India could invite Pakistan to participate in the 'Dosti' SAR exercise held annually between India and The Maldives. In time, this may become a regular feature and gather support of the other countries of the region and may develop in shape and concept like Joint Exercises Trincomalee of the 1950s and 1960s.
4. In this phase, the ICG and MSA ships at sea could coordinate their patrols and searches at sea and exchange operational information regarding smuggling, narcotics, and gun-running on designated radio frequencies. This phase could also include an agreement on monitoring fishing activities in the proposed ZoD.
5. At this stage, the two parties could establish communications between the ICG and MSA headquarters at Mumbai and Karachi and share data regarding pollution control, protection

of marine environment, and disaster management. This would go a long way towards getting an overall picture of the activities in the area of concern.

6. In time, the two countries could consider setting up Maritime Rapid Response Centres, linked to each other, with adequate and mandatory powers to board and inspect various types of craft for operations like anti-smuggling and anti-gun-running. Similarly, tankers passing through the area could also be inspected for anti-pollution operations.

According to Ghosh (2008), existing maritime CBMs between India and Pakistan, as gleaned from overall military agreements that have been signed, are as follows:

- It has been agreed that the navies of India and Pakistan will avoid holding major military manoeuvres and exercises in close proximity. Also, the strategic direction of the primary force being exercised will not be directed towards the other side and will not involve any logistic build-up close to it.
- The schedule of any major exercise involving six or more ships of the size of destroyer/frigate or above, exercising in company and crossing into each other's EEZ, will constitute a major exercise.
- The schedule of major exercises should be transmitted in writing to the other side through diplomatic channels at least 30 days in advance.
- Information on the type of exercise area, duration, and type of formations participating should be intimated. (In case of naval and air force exercises, only type, level, and area are required while exercises by the army require more information.)
- Naval ships and submarines are to keep a distance of 3 NM from each other so as to avoid accidents while operating in international waters.
- The aircraft of either country will refrain from 'buzzing' surface units of the other country in international waters.
- Military combat aircraft, helicopters, bomber reconnaissance, and jet trainers should not come within 10 km of each other

from the Air Defence Identification Zones (ADIZs) except in some special cases. However, unarmed aircraft and helicopters are permitted to come within 1,000 m from the ADIZ and each other's airspace.

With regard to the infraction of these CBMs, it has been noted that Pakistan naval ground aircraft have often been known to 'shadow' and 'buzz' Indian warships that exercise in the Arabian Sea and the Persian Gulf. This has led to Sea Harriers operating from the Indian aircraft carrier *INS Viraat* being used repeatedly to warn off Pakistan's snooping P3C Orions or Atlantiques. On the other hand, it has also been noted that the CBM on advance notification of major exercises is generally adhered to by both sides to prevent any escalation in maritime tension. It has been argued that, on the whole, notwithstanding numerous irritants, a cynical approach to the entire effort of observing the spirit of CBMs would be grossly erroneous, and that a positive spirit should be adopted while investigating and mutually resolving incidents of infractions.

Ghosh (2008) suggests a further set of CBMs, including (1) reciprocal visits and exchanges of high-level naval delegations; (2) establishment of new telecommunication channels and upgrading of existing ones; (3) direct talks between navies on the evolution of an INCSEA type agreement; (4) cooperation on environmental issues; (5) management of marine resources and reciprocal fishing rights; and (6) cooperation on non-military issues such as piracy and drug/gun-running.

He also suggests the following measures to facilitate the incremental nature of existing and proposed CBMs: (1) participation in joint and multilateral peacekeeping/enforcement operations; (2) cooperation in joint humanitarian operations with respect to natural disasters; (3) reciprocal maritime training; (4) cooperation on hydrographic surveys; and (5) increased shipping contact.

Many of these proposals for maritime CBMs have been made in the context of an India–Pakistan peace process, which held sway from about February 2004 till the November 2008 terrorist attacks on Mumbai. Soon after the attacks, it was established that they were carried out by Pakistani nationals infiltrating into

India by sea. According to the confessions of others arrested in connection with the attacks, Pakistan's intelligence agency Inter-Services Intelligence (ISI) also allegedly played a key role in the attacks, which were a major setback for the peace process. In an interview with the author, Commodore C. Uday Bhaskar of the National Maritime Foundation (NMF), New Delhi stated that while maritime cooperation with Pakistan was certainly desirable, its potential was limited because it depended on how Pakistan cooperated with India's effort to prosecute those responsible for the Mumbai attacks (Bhaskar 2011). Nevertheless, one must note that the Indian and Pakistani foreign secretaries met at Thimphu, Bhutan, in February 2011 and decided to take the dialogue process forward (Dikshit 2011). A media report has quoted a senior Indian government official involved in repairing ties with Pakistan as saying that 'the new talks are in effect the formal resumption of the composite dialogue', referring to the 2004 peace initiative (Mukherjee 2011). In an interview on the Indian television channel News X in April 2011, India's then Foreign Secretary Nirupama Rao (currently Ambassador of India to the US) stated that, over the following months, India and Pakistan would hold a series of meetings on numerous issues including the Sir Creek dispute. Arguably, these recent developments indicate that India and Pakistan are resuming cordial relations, seeking to get over the tension created by the November 2008 Mumbai attacks, and that several maritime CBMs discussed above are resuming relevance.

INDIA–SRI LANKA MARITIME COOPERATION

In December 2006, the NMF organized a seminar on India–Sri Lanka maritime cooperation. Participants included several retired and serving officials in their personal capacities from both countries, so this seminar can be seen as a Track II initiative. The presented papers have been published in Vohra and Srivatsan (2008). This section will examine India–Sri Lanka maritime cooperation in economic cooperation; fisheries; and non-military/non-traditional security cooperation.

Economic Cooperation

India liberalized its economy in 1991 and Sri Lanka had done so much earlier in 1978. With the liberalization of their economies, trade between two countries began increasing, and a free trade agreement was signed in 1998. Till 2003, India's trade with Sri Lanka doubled while Sri Lanka's trade with India grew sixfold. This agreement may have set an example for other countries in South Asia to promote greater economic cooperation through SAFTA. The main items exported from India to Sri Lanka are oilmeal, fruit and vegetables, marine products, raw cotton, leather and goods, drugs, pharmaceuticals, dyes, intermediaries and coal tar chemicals, toiletries, rubber products, glass, ceramics, cement, plastic and linoleum products, residual chemical and allied products, metal goods, machinery and instruments, transport equipment, iron and steel, primary and semi-finished steel, and yarn fabrics. The main items exported from Sri Lanka to India are spices, pulses, coconut products, graphite, natural rubber, organic chemicals, precious and semi-precious stones, artificial resins and plastic materials, pulp and paper, furnace oil and petroleum products, and tea. Apart from the official trade, however, unofficial trade is also reported. In the early days of Independence, contraband trade was a two-way flow, with significant quantities of goods being smuggled. While illicit trade took place by various means, smuggling by boat through the Palk Straits was one of the most prominent modes. The town of Velvettiturai on the northern coast of Sri Lanka, close to India, gained notoriety for smuggling activities between Sri Lanka and India and beyond. Recently, arms and ammunition, consumer goods, and drugs have been smuggled. The smuggling of arms, ammunition, and drugs will be dealt with in the sub-section on non-military/non-traditional security cooperation. With regard to smuggling of consumer goods, illegal trade has been rampant through coastal areas of Beruwala, Kalutara, Colombo, Wattala, Negombo, Puttalam, Kalpitiya, Mannar, Point Pedro, Mullaitivu as well as Velvettiturai on the Sri Lankan side, and coastal areas of Tamil Nadu and Kerala states on the Indian side. Reportedly, about eight boats worth of contraband trade takes place between

Sri Lanka and India everyday. Both countries would do well to realize that further relaxation of trade restrictions by abolishing tariffs and other barriers would minimize contraband trade (Raju & Keethaponcalan 2006: 71–5).

Fisheries

The fisheries issue in India–Sri Lanka relations is intertwined with their maritime boundary (Map 3), demarcated through agreements in 1974 and 1976. The 1974 agreement has two clauses relating to the rights of Indian fishermen. Article 5 of this agreement maintains that, 'subject to the foregoing, the Indian fishermen and pilgrims will enjoy access to visit Kachchativu as hitherto and will not be required by Sri Lanka to obtain travel documents or visas for these

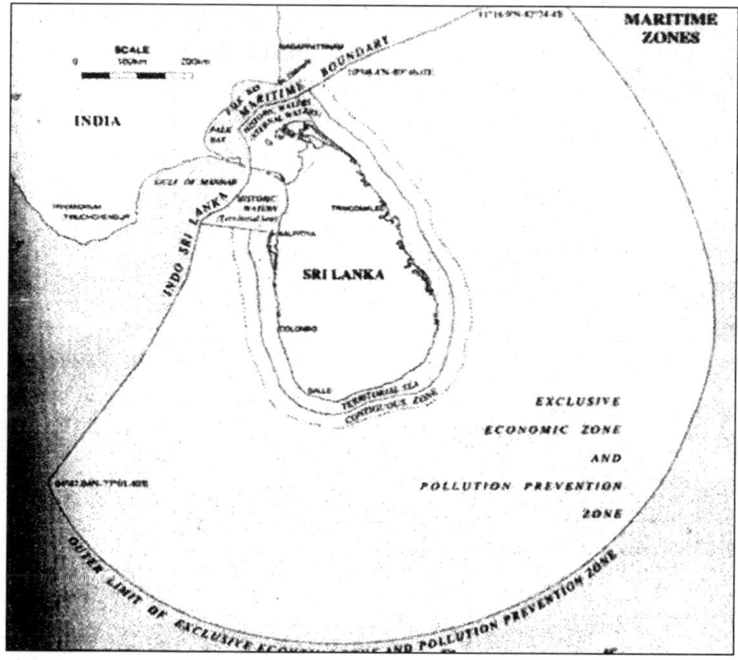

Source: Amarasiri, Wijayananda and Wijesuriya (2008: 72).

Map 3: India–Sri Lanka Maritime Boundary

purposes'. Article 6 states that, 'the vessels of Sri Lanka and India will enjoy in each other's waters such rights as they have enjoyed therein'. These two clauses may have given rise to the belief in India that Indian fishermen had the right to fish around the island of Kachchativu. However, this issue was legally laid to rest by the 1976 agreement and an exchange of letters between India and Sri Lanka at the time. In this exchange of letters, the Indian foreign secretary wrote to his Sri Lankan counterpart, stating:

> The fishing vessels of and fishermen of India shall not engage in fishing in the historic waters, the territorial sea and the exclusive economic zone of Sri Lanka nor shall the fishing vessels and fishermen of Sri Lanka engage in fishing in historic waters, territorial sea and the exclusive economic zone of India, without express permission of Sri Lanka or India, as the case may be. . . . (Raju & Keethaponcalan 2006: 22, 25)

However, Suryanarayan (2008: 26) has pointed out that these agreements were signed without considering the sensitivities of the people and government of Tamil Nadu and that, as a result, the Palk Bay has become a conflict zone. After winning the Tamil Nadu state elections in May/June 2011, chief minister of Tamil Nadu, J. Jayalalithaa, has reiterated her demand that the fishermen of Tamil Nadu be allowed to fish in the waters around Kachchativu. From Sri Lanka's point of view, since the military defeat of LTTE in May 2009, the problem is that northern Sri Lankan fishermen who were earlier not allowed to fish in many northern areas for security reasons are now allowed to, but they find that these fishing grounds have been taken over by fishermen from Tamil Nadu. The fisheries issue between India and Sri Lanka also has to do with the very nature of fishing—fish do not respect national boundaries and so, in their pursuit of fish, fishermen too are forced to transgress national boundaries. This is a challenge in relations between many coastal states. Not only do Indian fishermen cross into Sri Lankan waters—Sri Lankan fishermen too cross into Indian waters. In February 2011 alone, Sri Lanka arrested and then released 136 Indian fishermen (Bandara 2011a). Around the same time, in February/March 2011, India released 102 arrested Sri Lankan fishermen (Times Online 2011).

To deal with this problem *in tandem*, India and Sri Lanka set up a Joint Working Group on Fisheries in 2005. It met at New Delhi in April 2005, at Colombo in January 2006, and at New Delhi in March 2011. In October 2008, India and Sri Lanka issued a Joint Statement on Fishing Arrangements, which states that keeping in mind the humanitarian and livelihood dimensions of the fishermen issue, India and Sri Lanka have agreed to put in place practical arrangements to deal with bonafide Indian and Sri Lankan fishermen crossing the International Maritime Boundary Line (IMBL). Further, they agreed that there would be no firing at Indian fishing vessels, that Indian fishing vessels would carry valid registration/permit, and that fishermen would carry valid identity cards issued by the Government of Tamil Nadu. India and Sri Lanka also agreed to sustain discussions, initiated in 2005, on a proposed MoU on development and cooperation in the field of fisheries (MEA India 2008). Reportedly, the measures put in place by the October 2008 arrangement led to a remarkable drop in the number of arrests of Indian fishermen by the Sri Lankan authorities, from nearly 1500 in 2008 to only 34 in 2010; moreover, there were no incidents of killings in 2009 and 2010 (*Daily Mirror* 2011). However, in January 2011, two Tamil Nadu fishermen were killed in Sri Lankan waters. Following these incidents, Nirupama Rao made a high-profile visit to Sri Lanka and held discussions with top officials. Sri Lankan authorities emphasized that it was their consistent policy to treat all fishermen, including Indians, who cross into Sri Lankan waters in a humanitarian manner. The Sri Lankan side stressed further that, given the very close bilateral relationship between the two countries, any development impacting on the well-being of the Indian fishing community, pursuing its livelihood in the waters between the two countries, is of utmost concern to Sri Lanka. It also agreed to thoroughly investigate the incidents that led to the death of the two Indian fishermen (MEA India 2011a). Reporting to the Sri Lankan parliament on the investigations into these incidents, Prof. Peiris has said that there were no Sri Lanka Navy vessels in the vicinity of the locations of the alleged incidents (Indrajith 2011). Meanwhile, following the arrest of 136 Indian fishermen by Sri Lankan authorities in February 2011, India's

Minister of External Affairs S.M. Krishna pointed out to the Indian parliament the need for Indian fishermen to be conscious of Sri Lankan sensitivities and of not crossing the IMBL (Narayan 2011).

In the third meeting of the joint working group, the two sides noted that given the socio-economic and livelihood dimensions of the issue, there was need to enhance cooperation by building on earlier agreements. They agreed to discuss arrangements based on the current situation to bolster the safety, security, and livelihoods of the fishermen. Both sides welcomed the visit of a group of Indian fishermen from Tamil Nadu to Sri Lanka in March 2011. They called on Sri Lanka's Minister of Fisheries and Aquatic Resources, Minister of Small and Traditional Industries, and their counterparts from Sri Lanka's Northern Province. Recalling the initiatives taken in August 2010 by fishermen of both countries, where a Sri Lankan fishermen delegation had visited India, both sides agreed to foster greater understanding between their fishermen and fishermen associations. Noting the invitation extended by the Indian fishermen to their Sri Lankan counterparts, the two sides agreed that a reciprocal visit to India would be important to take this process forward. Both sides also discussed the various regulatory measures being put in place to manage the fishery resources in their respective waters. They noted the growing importance of fisheries to the livelihood of coastal communities in northern Sri Lanka, and agreed on the need for a roadmap to ensure resource sustainability, livelihood, and safety and security of the fishermen of both countries (MEA India 2011b).

Sri Lanka is also reported to be in the process of introducing, with assistance from Japan, a vessel monitoring system to alert its fishermen when they stray beyond its maritime territory. When this system is in place, fishermen would be alerted through signals (Bandara & De Chickera 2010).

Non-Military/Non-Traditional Security

For the three decades prior to 2009, the LTTE's activities constituted a major non-traditional security challenge in the vicinity of India and Sri Lanka. In many instances, India and Sri Lanka attempted to cooperate in the maritime domain to deal with this challenge, with varied success. During 1987–90, the terms of the Indo–Sri Lanka Agreement of 1987 specifically provided the Indian Navy the role of 'cooperating with the Sri Lankan Navy in preventing Tamil militant activities from affecting Sri Lanka'. However, this cooperation was not implemented effectively (Roy-Chaudhury 1998: 273). More recently, in 2006, India successfully stepped up intelligence cooperation with Sri Lanka, enabling the latter's navy to destroy two LTTE ships engaged in smuggling weapons (Suryanarayan 2008: 49).

Samarasinghe (2008: 102–4) highlights links between terror-ism and activities such as drug trafficking, poaching, and illicit seaborne immigration. With large profit margins, drug trafficking is by far the most lucrative means of generating funds to fuel ever-growing terrorist activities and insurgencies in the Indian Ocean region. Thus narco-terrorism has become a major security concern for a littoral state like India, which has emerged as a transit point for most drugs that originate in bordering countries. Poaching by south Indian fishermen in and around the shallow water reefs in northern Sri Lanka has often provided cover for terrorists to undertake logistics missions. Illicit migration is a long-standing issue and a major challenge to regional stability. The potential for terrorists to take advantage of human smuggling attempts to circumvent border security measures poses less risky alternatives for unlawful entry into India and Sri Lanka.

While the LTTE was militarily defeated in May 2009, at the time of writing, many media reports have surfaced about the possible continuation of LTTE activities. According to one, in February 2011, Indian central intelligence agencies had communicated specific inputs to the Tamil Nadu police that suspected LTTE cadres had conspired to attack Very Very Important Persons during the Tamil Nadu Assembly elections. Highly placed intelligence sources apparently confirmed to *The Hindu* that India's home ministry had sent alert messages that some LTTE cadres had arrived in Tamil Nadu; they were engaged in a training programme at an unknown location, and were procuring weapons and explosive substances to execute their plan. While claiming that LTTE men in the custody of the Sri Lankan army had revealed significant presence of their cadre at Valasaravakkam in Chennai, sources said that some prominent members of the LTTE's finance and air wings had sneaked into Tamil Nadu. Members of its suicide squad had reached Nagercoil on the Tamil Nadu coast in the guise of refugees accompanying aged or injured Sri Lankan Tamils. Clandestine sailings of the LTTE and frequent arrival of refugees with help of illegal boat operators had exposed the vulnerability of the Tamil Nadu coast, the sources said. The Indian police had also intercepted a couple of clandestine boat operators who organized the transport of Sri Lankan Tamil refugees to Australia. There was information about former LTTE cadres organizing human smuggling of Sri Lankan Tamils staying in Tamil Nadu as refugees to Australia and Canada. The same newspaper report, however, quoted senior Indian police officers, including the Director-General of Tamil Nadu Police, Letika Saran, as ruling out the possibility of LTTE cadre regrouping in Tamil Nadu and negating the presence of LTTE cadre in Tamil Nadu. Senior Indian police officers were further quoted as saying that they would continue to be vigilant of any suspicious activity along the Tamil Nadu coast, and that they were in the process of following up on intelligence inputs (*Daily News* 2011b).

In March 2011, during a debate on the extension of the state of emergency in Sri Lanka, Prime Minister D.M. Jayaratne claimed that intelligence reports indicated that LTTE guerillas were training at three separate locations in Tamil Nadu with the objective of assassinating Indian political leaders as well as re-establishing themselves in Sri Lanka. The Indian government immediately lodged an official protest with the Sri Lankan government regarding this speech. Indian officials went on record to deny the existence of such LTTE camps in Tamil Nadu, saying that there were no LTTE elements operating in Tamil Nadu. In the face of this denial, Jayaratne retracted his statement, claiming that it was based on incorrect information taken from news reports in two newspapers (Bandara 2011b; *The Sunday Times* 2011). Despite this minor diplomatic incident, media reports on the persistence of LTTE activity have continued to surface. In March 2011,

Sri Lankan newspapers announced several incidents of recovery of large hauls of weapons in northern and eastern Sri Lanka by security forces (Dias 2011a, 2011c, 2011d, 2011e). In the same month, explosives and detonating devices were reported to have been found on a public bus transporting passengers from Jaffna to Colombo (Dias 2011b). According to another media report in May 2011, a Canada-bound container was detained at Colombo port because it had several cartons of printed propaganda material of the LTTE. It quoted a senior Sri Lankan police officer as saying that, according to investigations, these cartons had arrived in Colombo via Chennai (Malalasekera 2011). This spate of media attention indicates that, diplomatic wrangling apart, it is extremely important that India and Sri Lanka cooperate in staying vigilant about sustained LTTE activity. Samarasinghe's (2008: 120) call for a bilateral agreement on cooperative maritime security is relevant. He points out the need for broader regional cooperation in the Indian Ocean and South Asia in combating terrorism and other related non-military/non-traditional security threats. He offers a comparison of maritime law enforcing capacities and resources of South Asian nations (Graph 1), for an analysis to consider resource/burden sharing and capacity building in the region. The overwhelming preponderance of Indian capacity and resources in this regard suggests that India is well-suited to play a leadership role in such cooperation.

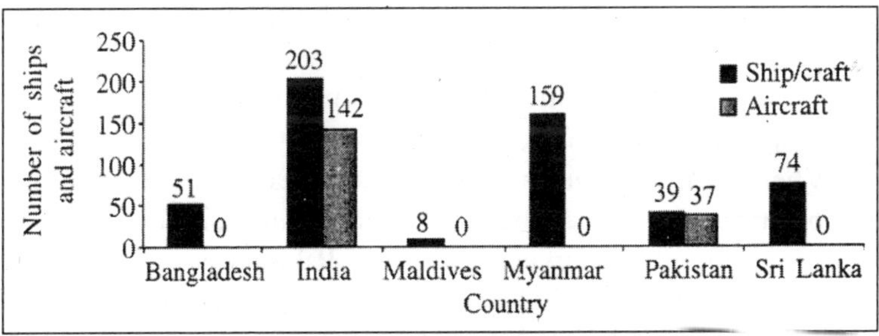

Source: Samarasinghe (2008: 120).

GRAPH 1: MARITIME LAW ENFORCEMENT CAPACITIES AND RESOURCES OF SOUTH ASIAN NATIONS

CONCLUSION

CBMs are probably the best and surest ways to enhance trust in a gradual incremental fashion between neighbouring nations that share adversarial relations. Given the unique geostrategic dynamics of India–Pakistan relations, a lot has already been done in this direction. However, the efficacy of any CBM is only as good as the 'observance will' of the concerned parties. Hence, prior to enhancing the sheer number of agreements and their clauses, it may be more beneficial to undertake a true trend analysis of the performance patterns of these agreements. In the bilateral context, while both governments have focused acutely on 'talks' on matters such as the nuclear issue and opening of borders via bus services, maritime subjects need greater attention since they form the easiest agenda for enhancing confidence. After all, as the old saying goes, 'the seas unite but the land divides' (Ghosh 2008: 37).

There is a greater need to enhance mutual cooperation between India and Sri Lanka on maritime security, through measures such as joint naval patrolling, control of smuggling and piracy, and strengthening of communication networks. With cooperation, both countries can improve shipbuilding, weather forecasting, preventing pollution, and combating maritime terrorism. Apart from such measures, there is great potential for enhancing and institutionalizing economic cooperation in the exploration and exploitation of marine resources in the Indian Ocean waters. A few steps have already been initiated by both countries to extend cooperation in some areas. Yet, a more organized thrust is needed to enhance and institutionalize maritime cooperation (Raju & Keethaponcalan 2006: 77).

When comparing India–Pakistan and India–Sri Lanka maritime cooperation efforts, one must bear in mind some contrasts. First, the maritime boundary between India and Pakistan is undemarcated while the one between India and Sri Lanka is demarcated. Second, trade between India and Pakistan is languishing while trade between India and Sri Lanka is flourishing. Some other things also need to be pointed out. First, even though the India–Sri Lanka maritime boundary is demarcated, Tamil Nadu—an Indian state neighbouring Sri Lanka—continues to insist on the right of its fishermen to fish in the waters around the island of Kachchativu, which the Indian government has acknowledged as belonging to Sri Lanka by the 1974 and 1976 agreements between the two countries. Second, a substantial amount of smuggling of consumer goods occurs between India and Pakistan as well as between India and Sri Lanka and, for both countries, trade liberalization is one counter to this contraband trade. Looking at similarities in India–Pakistan and India–Sri Lanka maritime cooperation efforts, what strikes one are the areas of fisheries and non-military/non-traditional security cooperation. In the approach to fisheries cooperation, there are many similarities. First, in both efforts, given the livelihood dimension of fishermen crossing over into the other country's waters, the issue is regarded as a humanitarian issue, and there is agreement that bonafide fishermen and their vessels arrested while in the other country's waters need to be repatriated as soon as possible. Second, both countries are keen on involving the fishermen's associations in their efforts to manage the problem. Third, both agendas mention the use of the technology of a vessel monitoring system to warn fishermen when they are straying into the other country's waters. While some of these issues are best handled bilaterally, given the highly migratory nature of fish stocks, some level of multilateralization can be helpful.

With regard to non-military/non-traditional security cooperation, both are keen on enhancing naval and coast guard cooperation to combat activities such as maritime terrorism and smuggling of arms, drugs, and humans. In fact, in an interview with the author, Ambassador Shyam Saran, a former foreign secretary of India and currently Chairman of the Research and Information System for Developing Countries (RIS), opined that India would be comfortable with multilateralizing its bilateral cooperation efforts with Pakistan and Sri Lanka in areas such as fisheries and non-military/non-traditional security. Based on this comparative analysis, this study argues that fisheries and non-military/non-traditional security issues might be profitably included in the evolving contemporary agenda for South Asian maritime cooperation.

Conclusion

Thinking about ocean space in terms of military strategy largely involves thinking about 'using' it by actual or threatened force, in the interest of one country or group of countries, against the interest of another country or group of countries. The LOSC 1982 can be thought of as an attempt to provide a set of rules aimed at peacefully 'regulating the use' of ocean space in the interest of all countries. The greater the link between a country's 'national economy' and the 'international' or 'regional' economy, the greater will be the importance of 'economic SLOC' to it. However, below the threshold of 'total war', a country is unlikely to exhaust its stockpiles of necessary materials to sustain a war effort. So, even if a country's economy is closely linked to the international or regional economy, below the threshold of 'total war' 'economic SLOC' may not be of crucial importance to a country's war effort, whereas in a condition of 'total war', 'economic SLOC' are certain to be of vital importance. Given that ships execute most of the international trade, sea lanes are vital to the functioning of the international or regional economy. Military strategy prescribes convoys and patrolling as ways for a country to secure vital SLOC. In a context of shared sea lanes, however, securing one's own SLOC can make those of another country insecure. The LOSC 1982 and other related institutional mechanisms for international cooperation seek to provide a system of regulations to make sea lanes secure for all countries. Military strategic prescriptions for securing SLOC/sea lanes—such as convoys and patrolling—should be subsumed within such a system of regulations in the form of joint multilateral operations. Alongside inter-state conflict, terrorism-at-sea and piracy have emerged as significant threats to the security of SLOC/sea lanes in recent years.

The LOSC 1982 places considerable emphasis on regional and international cooperation in maritime affairs. Its provisions relevant to such cooperation are as follows (Roy-Chaudhury 1998: 259–60):

- Article 98 on SAR operations requires states to promote the establishment, operation, and maintenance of an effective SAR service, and to cooperate where necessary with neighbouring states for this purpose.
- Article 100 on anti-piracy requires states to cooperate in the repression of piracy on the high seas.
- Article 108 on illicit drug trafficking requires states to cooperate in the suppression of illicit trafficking in narcotic drugs engaged in by ships on the high seas.
- Article 192 on environmental protection obliges states to protect and preserve the marine environment.
- Article 194 on anti-pollution requires states to take all measures to prevent, reduce, and control pollution of the marine environment.
- Article 276 on science and technology calls for the establishment of regional marine scientific and technological research centres.
- Article 277 describes the functions of these centres.

In the context of South Asia, Alam (1997) proposed the establishment of a SAARC CMC. Being a Bangladeshi naval officer, his idea was for Bangladesh to table such a proposal within SAARC. While nothing much appears to have emerged directly from this proposal, it gives us a fairly comprehensive idea of what South Asian maritime cooperation could look like and how we can start operationalizing it. It is also important to note many related developments. With regard to cooperation in non-military/non-traditional security areas such as prevention of drug smuggling and terrorism, SAARC had set up SDOMD and STOMD in 1992 and 1995, respectively. Since 2007, SAARC has worked to strengthen both these bodies. At the third meeting of the national focal points of SDOMD, held at Islamabad in June 2010, Pakistan offered to strengthen the body by making a one-time financial/material assistance and to prepare a concept paper on interaction between SAARC and the UNODC, to be considered by all member states. Further, the governments of Bangladesh, Pakistan, and Sri Lanka offered training courses/programmes in fields related to narcotics and drugs. Realizing the importance of learning from each other's experiences, the member states agreed to submit country reports on the drug situations in their countries to the SDOMD and also share information. At the STOMD's third meeting, held at Islamabad in June 2010, member states decided to share real-time information and exchange data on terrorist photographs, incidents, and profiles with the STOMD. With regard to the marine environment, the SAARC set up the SCZMC in 2005. It promotes cooperation in planning, management, and sustainable development of coastal zones, including research, training, and awareness generation. In 2007, the SAARC Coastal Zone Management Action Plan gained the approval of the concerned decision-making bodies. This document provides a comprehensive agenda for cooperation in regional CZM. Further, at the time of writing this paper, The Maldives is in the process of preparing a concept paper on developing principles of modern law relating to maritime security and piracy to be circulated to all SAARC member countries. At the same time, it is important to keep in mind the possibility that South Asian maritime cooperation could be institutionalized independently of SAARC while being complementary to it. In this connection, there is much to learn from the establishment and operation of the JCLEC in the neighbouring Southeast Asian region; it has been set-up independently of ASEAN yet works closely with bodies linked to the latter. Similarly, any prospective organization for South Asian maritime cooperation set-up independently of SAARC could also work closely with it.

When thinking about multilateral maritime cooperation in South Asia, two important points must be taken into account. First, there has been considerable effort at maritime cooperation between India and Pakistan, as well as between India and Sri Lanka, particularly in the last few years; both these bilateral cooperative relationships are ongoing ones. Such bilateral maritime cooperation among South Asian countries could be used as a basis for South Asian multilateral maritime cooperation, with India playing a central and leading role. Second, it is important to locate South Asia as a continental sub-region within the Indian Ocean maritime region. The Bay of Bengal, which is a sub-region of the Indian Ocean maritime region, links the two continental sub-regions of South Asia and Southeast Asia. The Arabian Sea, another sub-region of the Indian Ocean maritime region, links South Asia to the continental sub-region of West Asia (or the Middle East). This configuration implies that multilateral maritime cooperation in South Asia may well overlap with multilateral maritime cooperation in West Asia (or the Middle East) and in Southeast Asia. If one thinks institutionally, this translates into the realization that South Asian maritime cooperation—within or outside SAARC—may well have to be coordinated with maritime cooperation within the GCC as well as within ASEAN.

This study seeks to argue that India's bilateral maritime co-operation with other South Asian countries such as Pakistan and Sri Lanka can be used as the building block of South Asian multilateral maritime cooperation. It is notable that some writings on both India–Pakistan and India–Sri Lanka maritime cooperation have suggested the expansion of bilateral cooperation to the regional level. Ansari and Vohra (2003: 38) suggest expansion of the annual SAR exercises between India and The Maldives to include Pakistan, and thence other countries of the region as well. Siddiqa-Agha (2000: 29) proposes that India–Pakistan cooperation on combating smuggling of drugs and humans could include other regional states. The eighth symposium on Confidence and Cooperation in South Asian Waters held in June 2011 has suggested that the focus of the symposium be broadened from it's hitherto one of India–Pakistan maritime cooperation to broader regional cooperation (CFPS 2012). Samarasinghe (2008: 120) calls for expansion of India–Sri Lanka maritime security cooperation to combat terrorism and other related non-military/non-traditional security threats to include other countries of the Indian Ocean and South Asia. Looking at India–Pakistan trade cooperation, it emerges that open trade with

India would reduce the cost of foodstuffs in Pakistan by 20–30 per cent. Ansari and Vohra (2003: 24) have argued that the revision of the India–Pakistan Shipping Protocol of 1975 would remove impediments to the free movement of goods and cargo, and pave the way for booming cross-border trade. It is encouraging to note the unanimous decision taken by the Pakistani cabinet to grant Most Favoured Nation trade status to India (*Daily News* 2011c). Greater open trading between India and Pakistan would also be of much benefit to the progress of SAFTA. In turn, given the fact that much of international trade is facilitated by ship, the increase of intra-regional trade in South Asia would provide one of the best rationales for South Asian maritime cooperation. Further, the progress of liberalization of trade in South Asia could also minimize the intra-regional smuggling of consumer goods.

This study has attempted to identify common areas in India–Pakistan and India–Sri Lanka bilateral maritime cooperation efforts and use those lowest common denominators as the starting points for South Asian multilateral maritime cooperation. One could criticize this method for restricting the pace of efforts at South Asian multilateral maritime cooperation to the pace of efforts at India–Pakistan bilateral maritime cooperation, the most troubled bilateral relationship in this context. In response, one would do well to keep in mind the time-tested saying: 'Slow but steady wins the race.' Through comparative analysis of efforts at India–Pakistan and India–Sri Lanka bilateral maritime cooperation, fisheries and non-military/non-traditional security cooperation emerged as areas common to both; this study argues that these areas ought to be included in the evolving agenda for South Asian maritime cooperation. It has also emerged that, in regard to non-military/non-traditional security cooperation, with the overwhelming preponderance of Indian capacity in terms of vessels, aircraft and training facilities in South Asia, India is positioned well to play a regional leadership role. At the same time, given the international character of the maritime domain, efforts must be made to co-ordinate evolving South Asian maritime cooperation with similar efforts in the neighbouring regions and the world.

Finally, this study would like to recall its limitations and present suggestions for further research. An effort to build South Asian multilateral maritime cooperation based on India's bilateral maritime cooperation with other South Asian countries ought also to include India's maritime cooperation with Bangladesh and The Maldives. The lack of secondary literature on these subjects is a challenge. In an interview with the author, Ambassador Saran revealed that the problem of fishermen crossing over into each other's maritime territory also exists between India and Bangladesh. During India's Prime Minister Dr Manmohan Singh's visit to Bangladesh in September 2011, the two nations signed an MoU on Cooperation in the Field of Fisheries (MEA India 2011c).

India's maritime cooperation with The Maldives also seems to be going from strength to strength. In 2006, India gifted the patrol vessel *INS Tillanchang* to The Maldives. India and The Maldives regularly conduct a series of exercises called 'Dosti', involving maritime patrolling and rescue operations around The Maldives. Around the time of Indian defence minister A.K. Antony's visit to The Maldives in August 2009, India was slated to hand over to The Maldives one helicopter from the ICG and another from the Indian Navy. A project under discussion then was Indian assistance to The Maldives in setting up maritime surveillance and reconnaissance systems including radars on all its islands, to be networked with India's Coastal Command to create a seamless radar picture of common sea areas in the Arabian Sea. The ICG was to undertake regular air patrols in the southern Arabian Sea to help The Maldives manage the security of its waters (Sakhuja 2009). During Maldivian President Mohamed Nasheed's visit to New Delhi in February 2011, some effort seems to have gone into harmonizing Indian and Maldivian views on the Indian Ocean (*The Times of India* 2011). In an official meeting in July 2011 between an Indian delegation led by K. Mohandas, Secretary, Ministry of Shipping, and a Maldivian delegation led by Mohamed Latheef, Permanent Secretary, Ministry of Transport and Communication, the two nations decided to initiate work on a comprehensive bilateral maritime cooperation agreement (PIB 2011). As India's bilateral maritime cooperation with Bangladesh and The Maldives unfolds over the coming years, a fruitful research exercise would be to undertake a systematic comparison of bilateral maritime cooperation between India and each of the other four maritime South Asian countries, so as to contribute to the agenda for multilateral maritime cooperation in South Asia.

APPENDIX

SAARC Coastal Zone Management Action Plan[1]

1. *Noting* that oceans cover 70 per cent of the planet's surface area and coastal and marine environments contain diverse habitats that support an abundance of marine life; and that life in our seas produces a third of the oxygen that we breathe, offers a valuable source of protein and moderates global climatic change;
2. *Recognizing* that despite being home to 6 per cent of the world's coral reefs, providing a habitat to a critical source of food and livelihoods to millions of people; and notwithstanding the wealth of pelagic or open-ocean communities, deep-sea communities, mangrove forests and seagrass beds in the South Asian region, the achievements in sustainable management of these critical habitats have been inadequate;
3. *Recognizing* further that coastal and marine habitats in South Asia region are under threat from pollution, overexploitation of natural resources and unplanned coastal development and natural causes, which inflict heavy pressures on the resource base due to increased demands on marine and coastal resources across the region in the form of extractive processes for food, income generation, medicines, and building materials degrade coastal ecosystems in many locations;
4. *Mindful* that in 2003 the United Nations ranked South Asia region among the lowest in the world in terms of declared

[1] This document is reproduced from SCZMC (2007).

marine and coastal protected areas making the Indian Ocean perhaps the most poorly protected coastline/ocean;

5. *Noting* that marine and coastal biodiversity are priority work areas in a number of international and regional programmes; notably Convention on Biological Diversity (CBD), Convention on the Conservation of Migratory Species of Wild Animals (CMS), and The Indian Ocean–South East Asian (IOSEA) Marine Turtle Memorandum of Understanding;
6. *Recognizing* that the conservation of marine and coastal environment is specifically addressed in the Action Plan for the South Asian Regional Seas Programme and Programme of Work on Marine and Coastal Biodiversity under the CBD;
7. *Recognizing* that other international instruments, including the United Nations Convention on the Law of the Sea, the FAO Code of Conduct for Responsible Fisheries, the International Convention for the Prevention of Pollution from Ships (MARPOL), and the Convention on Biological Diversity (CBD), are relevant to conservation and sustainable utilization of the coastal and marine habitats;
8. *Recognizing* the SAARC Development Goals and the Millennium Development Goals (MDGs) that call for environmental sustainability to significantly reduce the loss of biological diversity;
9. *Noting* that existing regional organizations, South Asian Seas Programme, South Asian Cooperative Environment Programme operate programmes relevant to the conservation of the coastal and marine habitats;
10. *Noting* that environment has remained as an important agenda in the SAARC process as demonstrated by the SAARC Regional Study on the Causes and Consequences of Natural Disasters and the Protection and Preservation of the Environment, SAARC Plan of Action on Environment, the Colombo Declaration for a Common Environment Programme and the SAARC Environment Action Plan adopted by the 3rd meeting of the SAARC Environment Ministers (Male, 1997);
11. *Recognizing* the importance of concerted actions to conserve

coastal and marine habitats with activities related to the socio-economic development of the Member States;

12. *Acknowledging* the individual and collective responsibility of the Member States to address the threats posed to marine and coastal habitats, and for the conservation and management of marine and coastal habitats;
13. *Reaffirming* the importance of involving all the Member States, as well as relevant inter-governmental, non-governmental, community-based and private sector organizations, in co-operative conservation and management of coastal and marine habitats;
14. *Agreeing* that the Programme of Work on marine and coastal biological diversity should be applied and interpreted consistently with national laws, and wherever applicable, international law, including the United Nations Convention on the Law of the Sea;
15. *Agreeing* to pursue the actions set forth in this Action Plan, at national and regional levels, with coordination and follow up to be provided by the SCZMC to improve the conservation of marine and coastal environments in the South Asia region;
16. *Recognizing* the interdependence of economies within a common ecosystem and the relevance of coastal zone resources for all littoral states, coastal and non-coastal alike;
17. *Noting* in this context, that environmental interventions in a non-coastal littoral state affects the resources, lives and livelihood in littoral coastal states, and noting further, the common benefit of coastal zones resources for coastal and non-coastal states, especially in mitigating the impact of natural disasters; and adopts the SAARC Coastal Zone Management Activity Plan as set below:

RECOMMENDATIONS

#	Issues	Recommendations	Priority
1.	Enhancing regional environmental governance on coastal and related environmental issues	(a) Urge upon the Member States, who have not done so, to ratify/accede to relevant international environmental instruments, including: i. The International Convention for the Prevention of Pollution from Ships (MARPOL 73/78); ii. Convention on the Conservation of Migratory Species (CMS); iii. The Indian Ocean–South-East Asian Marine Turtle Memorandum of Understanding; iv. Global Ballast Water Programme; and v. Basel Convention on the Control of Transboundary Movements of Hazardous Wastes and their Disposal	-
		(b) Promote trans-boundary collaboration in implementing environmental standards.	-
2.	Strengthening national capacity to identify and combat invasive alien species	• Establish a regional clearing house mechanism on invasive alien species.	M
		• Develop a regional roster of experts on invasive alien species.	M
		• Develop national guidelines on management of ballast water.	M
		• Strengthen national capacity on marine invasive alien species.	H
		• Strengthen regional cooperation with relevant international organizations dealing with invasive alien species.	H
3.	Increasing capacity at the national level to deal with coastal zone management (CZM) and relevant issues	• Undertake a national capacity needs assessment for each Member State, both in the context of coastal and non-coastal states.	H
		• Identify training facilities related to CZM and related disciplines in Member States.	H

#	Issues	Recommendations	Priority
		• Compile coastal and marine habitats of the South Asian region.	H
		• Identify, at a national level, ecologically critical areas and endangered coastal and marine habitat and species and undertake conservation and management plans.	H
4.	Mitigating global impacts on coral reefs at a regional level	• Identify and collaborate with centres of excellence to collect and disseminate 'early warning' information on El Niño and other related impacts.	H
		• Establish an expert group network for sharing information and research on global impacts on coral reefs.	H
5.	Strengthening conservation of migratory species	• Encourage establishment of transboundary coastal and marine protected areas, with special priority to spawning grounds.	H
6.	Combating coastal erosion	• Establish a roster of experts on coastal erosion.	H
		• Increase capacity building in coastal engineering, coastal hydrodynamics and oceanography at national levels.	H
		• Identify and make available the regional tertiary institutions that conduct training in erosion protection fields.	H
		• Consider the impact of transboundary activities on coastal degradation, including deforestation and unplanned exploitation of resources.	-
7.	Protecting ecologically critical and endangered coastal areas and marine habitats and biodiversity	• Strengthen law enforcement to protect critical and endangered habitats and biodiversity.	H
		• Undertake assessment of status of coastal and marine habitats of the South Asian region.	H

#	Issues	Recommendations	Priority
8.	Addressing the lack of regional and national capacity on oil contingency planning	• Develop regional and national oil contingency plans.	H
		• Increase national and regional capacity in dealing with oil spills.	H
9.	Building regional capacity to undertake research and provide appropriate training in relation to CZM	• Design appropriate curriculum at secondary and tertiary levels to incorporate CZM issues and sustainable use of coastal resources.	M
		• Develop short- and long-term training programmes at appropriate educational training institutions on CZM issues and sustainable use of coastal resources.	M
		• Establish exchange programmes between various educational and research institutions undertaking research or training programmes to foster and facilitate experience sharing, knowledge exchange and capacity building.	M
10.	Reducing the impacts of aquaculture and marine culture on coastal and marine habitats	• Undertaking a study on good practices and lessons learnt in aquaculture and share the findings through workshops, seminars and exchange programmes between Member States.	M
11.	Increasing awareness on coastal and marine issues	• Establish a network of environmental writers in the print media to increase awareness on regional, coastal and marine issues.	–
		• Facilitate exchange programmes for radio and TV producers to produce public awareness programmes for radio and TV in Member States.	–

#	Issues	Recommendations	Priority
		• Provide, through the SAVE programme, documentaries on coastal and marine issues from Member States.	–
		• Urge upon Member States to initiate mass awareness campaigns on coastal and marine environmental issues.	–
		There is critical need to address the differential nature of awareness building in the coastal and non-coastal states.	
12.	Integrating non-coastal Member States in the implementation of the Action Plan	• Highlight the interconnectedness of environmental exigencies and interventions by all Member States on natural resources in South Asia, including coastal zone resources.	-
		• Organize core activities with a non-coastal state focus.	-

H = high priority; M = medium priority

PROPOSED IMPLEMENTATION STRATEGIES FOR THE SAARC COASTAL ZONE MANAGEMENT ACTION PLAN

- Recommend a round table of all donor/funding agencies/organizations to seek funding to finance the action plan.
- Incorporate recommended actions, where appropriate, into national policies, development plans and projects.
- Urge all Member States to develop national coastal zone management Action Plans before 2010.
- Identify national focal point(s) for each Member State to coordinate all activities in relation to this Action Plan at a national level.
- Mandate the SCZMC to coordinate and follow up on the implementation of the Action Plan.
- Integrate all Member States in this effort, with special initiatives to engage non-coastal Member States. Towards this end, consider holding the proposed round table in a non-coastal Member State.

Bibliography

Abyankar, J. (2001), 'Piracy and Ship Robbery: A Growing Menace', in A. Hamzah and A. Ogawa (eds), *Combating Piracy*, Kuala Lumpur: The Okazaki Institute [cited in Graham 2006: 56].

Ahmadzada, Azizuddin and Ghulam Dastgir (2011), personal interview, SAARC Secretariat, Kathmandu, Nepal, 19 April 2011.

Alam, Mohd Khurshed (1997), 'Regional Maritime Cooperation under the Auspices of South Asian Association for Cooperation (SAARC)', *Bangladesh Institute for International and Strategic Studies (BIISS) Journal*, vol. 18, no. 1, pp. 19–41.

Amarasiri, Champa, N.P. Wijayananda and H.P.T. Wijesuriya (2008), 'Marine Resource Exploitation: Building Partnerships', in Ravi Vohra and V. Srivatsan (eds), *India–Sri Lanka Maritime Cooperation: Opportunities and Challenges*, Regional Maritime Cooperation Series, New Delhi: National Maritime Foundation.

Anand, R.P. (1983), *Origin and Development of the Law of the Sea: History of International Law Revisited*, The Hague, Boston and London: Martinus Nijhoff Publishers.

Ansari, Hasan and Ravi Vohra (2003), 'Confidence Building Measures at Sea: Opportunities for India and Pakistan', *Cooperative Monitoring Centre Occasional Paper/33*, Albuquerque, NM: Cooperative Monitoring Centre, Sandia National Laboratories, available online at www.cmc.sandia.gov/cmc-papers/sand2004-0102.pdf, last accessed on 23 March 2011.

ASEAN (Association of Southeast Asian Nations) (2003), 'ARF Statement on Cooperation Against Piracy and Other Threats to Maritime Security', available online at www.aseansec.org/14838.htm, last accessed on 31 August 2004 [cited in Graham 2006: 54].

Bandara, Kelum (2011a), 'Indian Fishermen Return Home', *Daily Mirror*, 19 February 2011, available online at http://print.dailymirror.lk/news/front-page-news/36163.html, last accessed on 21 February 2011.

——— (2011b), 'India Rejects PM's Claims', *Daily Mirror*, 11 March 2011, available online at http://print.dailymirror.lk/news/front-page-news/37886.html, last accessed on 11 March 2011.

Bandara, Kelum and Gihan De Chickera (2010), 'Law of the Sea Not Properly Observed by India: Rajitha', *Daily Mirror*, 20 May 2010.

Bhaskar, C. Uday (2011), personal interview, National Maritime Foundation, New Delhi, India, 14 April 2011.

Blouin, J. (1989), 'Convoy or Defended Lanes', *Journal of Australian Naval Institute*, August 1989 [cited in Graham 2006: 45].

CFPS (Centre for Foreign Policy Studies) (2012), Dalhousie University, Halifax, 'Confidence and Cooperation in South Asian Waters', available online at http://centreforforeignpolicystudies.dal.ca/events/marsec_CCSAW.php, last accessed on 2 March 2012.

CoMC (Cooperative Monitoring Centre) (2002), Detailed Report on the Symposium on Confidence Building in South Asian Waters, Kuala Lumpur, Malaysia, May 2002 [cited in Ansari and Vohra 2003: 34].

Coulter, Daniel (1997), 'The Economics of SLOC Protection: An Overvalued Mission', a paper presented at the Eleventh International Conference on the Sea Lanes of Communication (SLOC) Studies, 17–18 November 1997, Tokyo [cited in Graham 2006: 48–50].

——— (1998), 'Hub Ports and Focal Points: New Entrants in the Maritime Security Lexicon', in A.L. Griffiths, R.H. Thomas and P.T. Haydon (eds), *The Changing Strategic Importance of International Shipping*, Halifax, Nova Scotia: Centre for Foreign Policy Studies, Dalhousie University [cited in Graham 2006: 50].

CID (Criminal Investigation Department) (*c.* 1992), Sri Lanka Police Department (Internal Document), 'Proposal to Establish a Unit to Assist Liaison Officers in the Exchange of Information to Combat Terrorism', Colombo.

——— (2001), Sri Lanka Police Department (Internal Document) 'SAARC Terrorist Offences Monitoring Desk (STOMD)', 27 December 2001, Colombo.

Daily Mirror (2011), 'Fishermen, Again', 28 January 2011, available online at http://print.dailymirror.lk/opinion1/34212.html, last accessed on 29 January 2011.

Daily News (2011a), 'Implementing SAARC Programmes: Sri Lanka Plays Leadership Role', 14 February 2011, available online at www.dailynews.lk/2011/02/14/news03.asp, last accessed on 14 February 2011.

——— (2011b), 'LTTE Threat for Indian VVIPs', 14 February 2011, available online at www.dailynews.lk/2011/02/14/sec01.asp, last accessed on 14 February 2011.

——— (2011c), 'Pakistan Grants India Most Favoured Nation Trade Status', 9 November 2011, 'Breaking News' Column (2 November 2011), available online at www.dailynews.lk/2011/11/09/cdnstory.asp?sid=20111102_02&imid=India_Parkisthan.jpg&dt=[November 02 2011], last accessed on 9 November 2011.

Dias, Supun (2011a), 'Thirty Three Anti-Personnel Mines Found in North', *Daily Mirror*, 12 March 2011, available online at http://print.dailymirror.lk/news/news/38012.html, last accessed on 14 March 2011.

——— (2011b), 'Explosives Found Under Seat of Colombo Bound Bus', *Daily Mirror*, 12 March 2011, available online at http://print.dailymirror.lk/news/news/38013.html, last accessed on 14 March 2011.

——— (2011c), 'Security Forces Recover More Weapons', *Daily Mirror*, 14 March 2011, available online at http://print.dailymirror.lk/news/news/38105.html, last accessed on 14 March 2011.

——— (2011d), 'STF Recovers Weapons in Vellamulliwaikkal', *Daily Mirror*, 17 March 2011, available online at http://print.dailymirror.lk/news/news/38458.html, last accessed on 17 March 2011.

——— (2011e), 'TNT and Anti Personnel Mines Recovered', *Daily Mirror*, 26 March 2011, available online at http://print.dailymirror.lk/news/news/39375.html, last accessed on 26 March 2011.

Dikshit, Sandeep (2011), 'India, Pakistan to Take Dialogue Process Forward', *The Hindu*, 7 February 2011, available online at www.hindu.com/2011/02/07/stories/2011020763881200.htm, last accessed on 10 February 2011.

D-maps.com (2012), 'Indian Ocean', available online at http://d-maps.com/m/indien/indien01.gif, last accessed on 29 February 2012.

Ghosh, P.K. (2008), 'Maritime Confidence Building Measures in South Asia: The Case of India and Pakistan', *Security And Terrorism Research Bulletin*, Issue 8, May 2008, available online at www.grc.ae/data/contents/uploads/Security_no_8_5831.pdf, last accessed on 28 November 2008.

Graham, Euan (2006), *Japan's Sea Lane Security: A Matter of Life and Death?*, London and New York: Routledge, Taylor and Francis Group.

Grove, E.J. (1993), 'Navies in Future Conflicts', in A. Bergin and H. Smith (eds), *Naval Power in the Pacific: Toward the Year 2000*,

Boulder, Colorado and London: Lynne Rienner [cited in Graham 2006: 47].

IOMOU (2012), Indian Ocean Memorandum of Understanding on Port State Control, available online at www.iomou.org/historymain.htm, last accessed on 2 March 2012.

Indrajith, Saman (2011), 'Govt. Must be Mindful of its Own', *The Island Online*, 25 February 2011, available online at www.island.lk/index.php?page_cat=article-details&page=article-details&code_title=19216, last accessed on 27 February 2011.

JCLEC (Jakarta Centre for Law Enforcement Cooperation) (2011), 'About JCLEC', available online at www.jclec.com/index.php?option=com_content&task=view&id=14&Itemid=28, last accessed on 12 January 2011.

Keohane, Robert O. and Joseph Nye (2001), *Power and Interdependence*, 3rd edn, New York: Longman.

Khan, Raja Muhammad (2011), 'Analyzing the South Asian Security', 10 September 2011, available online at http://maritimesecurity.asia/free-2/maritime-security-asia/analysing-the-south-asian-security/, last accessed on 19 December 2011.

Khan, Zillur R. (1991), *SAARC and the Superpowers*, Dhaka: University Press, cited in Mohd Khurshed Alam (1997), 'Regional Maritime Cooperation under the Auspices of South Asian Association for Cooperation (SAARC)', *BIISS Journal*, vol. 18, no. 1, p. 22 [cited in Alam 1997: 22].

Lehr, Peter (2005), 'Prospects for Multilateral Security Cooperation in the Indian Ocean: A Skeptical View', *Indian Ocean Survey*, vol. 1, no. 1, January–June 2005, pp. 1–15.

Malalasekera, Sarath (2011), 'Canada-Bound Container: CID Takes Over Probe', *Daily News*, 19 May 2011, available online at www.dailynews.lk/2011/05/19/sec01.asp, last accessed on 19 May 2011.

MEA (Ministry of External Affairs) India (2008), *India–Sri Lanka Joint Statement on Fishing Arrangements*, 26 October 2008, available online at http://meaindia.nic.in/mystart.php?id=530514308, last accessed on 19 June 2011.

——— (2011a), *Joint Statement During the Visit of Foreign Secretary Smt. Nirupama Rao to Sri Lanka*, 31 January 2011, available online at http://meaindia.nic.in/mystart.php?id=530517124, last accessed on 19 June 2011.

——— (2011b), *Meeting of India Sri Lanka JWG on Fisheries: Joint Press Statement*, 29 March 2011, available online at http://meaindia.nic.in/mystart.php?id=530517478, last accessed on 19 June 2011.

——— (2011c), *MOU Between India and Bangladesh on Cooperation in the Field of Fisheries*, 6 September 2011, available online at www.mea.gov.in/mystart.php?id=530518200, last accessed on 28 December 2011.

Mukherjee, Krittivas (2011), 'Report: India, Pakistan to Resume Peace Talks', available online at www.msnbc.msn.com/id/41504564/ns/world_news-south_and_central_asia, last accessed on 10 February 2011.

Nambiar, Satish (2009), 'Regional Security Cooperation in South Asia', in Harjeet Singh (ed.), *South Asia Defence and Strategic Yearbook 2009*, New Delhi: Pentagon Press.

Narayan, S. Venkat (2011), 'India Tells Her Fishermen: Respect SL Sensitivities, Do Not Cross MBL', *The Island Online*, 25 February 2011, available online at www.island.lk/index.php?page_cat=article-details&page=article-details&code_title=19204, last accessed on 27 February 2011.

Pinto, Christopher (1992), 'Maritime Security and the 1982 United Nations Convention on the Law of the Sea', in Josef Goldblatt (ed.), *Maritime Security: The Building of Confidence*, New York: United Nations.

PIB (Press Information Bureau), Government of India (2011), 'India and Maldives to Improve Bilateral Maritime Cooperation: Passenger-Cum-Cargo Ferry Service to Start Between Cochin and Male', available online at http://pib.nic.in/newsite/erelease.aspx?relid=73217, last accessed on 28 December 2011.

Raju, Adluri Subramanyam and S.I. Keethaponcalan (2006), 'Maritime Cooperation Between India and Sri Lanka', *RCSS Policy Studies 36*, Colombo: Regional Centre for Strategic Studies, and New Delhi: Manohar.

Roy-Chaudhury, Rahul (1998), 'Maritime and Naval Cooperation in the Indian Ocean', *Asian Strategic Review 1997-98*, New Delhi: Institute for Defence Studies and Analyses.

SAARC (South Asian Association for Regional Cooperation) (2010a), 'SAARC Drug Offences Monitoring Desk (SDOMD)', available online at www.saarc-sec.org/areaofcooperation/detail.php?activity_id=23, last accessed on 22 November 2010.

——— (2010b), 'SAARC Terrorist Offences Monitoring Desk (STOMD)', available online at www.saarc-sec.org/areaofcooperation/detail.php?activity_id=24, last accessed on 22 November 2010.

——— (2012a), 'Cooperation with Observers', available online at www.saarc-sec.org/Cooperation-with-Observers/13/, last accessed on 1 March 2012.

——— (2012b), 'South Asian Free Trade Area (SAFTA)', available online at www.saarc-sec.org/areaofcooperation/detail.php?activity_id=5, last accessed on 2 March 2012.

——— (2012c), 'Agreement on South Asian Free Trade Area (SAFTA)', available online at www.saarc-sec.org/uploads/document/SAFTA%20AGREEMENT_20110811115331.pdf, last accessed on 2 March 2012.

Sakhuja, Vijay (2001), 'Maritime Dimensions of Transnational Crime and Terrorism', in Jasjit Singh (ed.), *Reshaping Asian Security*, New Delhi: Knowledge World and Institute of Defence Studies and Analyses.

——— (2009), 'India and Maldives: Exploring Newer Vista for Cooperation', Indian Council of World Affairs, available online at www.icwa.in/pdfs/VPdoc_VP-IndiaAndMaldives.pdf, last accessed on 28 December 2011.

Samarasinghe, T.S.G. (2008), 'Sustainable Cooperative Security: Challenges and Options', in Ravi Vohra and V. Srivatsan (eds), *India–Sri Lanka Maritime Cooperation: Opportunities and Challenges*, Regional Maritime Cooperation Series, New Delhi: National Maritime Foundation.

Saran, Shyam (2011), personal interview, Research and Information System for Developing Countries, New Delhi, India, 14 April 2011.

SCZMC (SAARC Coastal Zone Management Centre) (2007), *SAARC Coastal Zone Management Action Plan*, SCZMC: Male.

——— (2011a), 'About SCZMC', available online at www.sczmc.org/about-sczmc/, last accessed on 19 July 2011.

——— (2011b), 'Inauguration', available online at www.sczmc.org/inauguration/, last accessed on 19 July 2011.

——— (2011c), 'Objectives', available online at www.sczmc.org/objectives/, last accessed on 19 July 2011.

Shipping Facts (2012), 'Shipping and World Trade: Overview', available online at www.marisec.org/shippingfacts//worldtrade/index.php, last accessed on 2 March 2012.

Siddiqa-Agha, Ayesha (2000), 'Maritime Cooperation between India and Pakistan: Building Confidence at Sea', *Cooperative Monitoring Centre Occasional Paper/18*, November 2000, Albuquerque, NM and Livermore, CA: Sandia National Laboratories, available online at www.osti.gov/bridge/servlets/purl/771482-w5sNgS/webviewable/771482.PDF, last accessed on 25 October 2008.

Singh, Jasjit (1984), *Indian Ocean in Global Strategies: Some Perspectives*, cited in Mohd. Khurshed Alam (1997), 'Regional Maritime Cooperation under the Auspices of South Asian Association for Cooperation (SAARC)', *BIISS Journal*, vol. 18, no. 1, p. 20 [cited in Alam 1997: 20].

Singh, K.R. (2004), 'India, Indian Ocean and Regional Maritime Cooperation', *International Studies*, vol. 41, no. 2, pp. 195–218.

Steinberg, Philip E. (2001), *The Social Construction of the Ocean*, Cambridge: Cambridge University Press.

Suryanarayan, V. (2008), 'India's Prognosis and Outlook', in Ravi Vohra and V. Srivatsan (eds), *India–Sri Lanka Maritime Cooperation: Opportunities and Challenges*, Regional Maritime Cooperation Series, New Delhi: National Maritime Foundation.

Tangredi, Sam J. (2002), 'Globalization and Sea Power: Overview and Context', in Sam J. Tangredi (ed.), *Globalization and Maritime Power*, Washington, D.C.: Institute for National Strategic Studies, National Defense University.

The Sunday Times (2011), 'India Makes Official Protest Over PM's Remarks', 13 March 2011, available online at http://sundaytimes.lk/110313/News/nws_03.html, last accessed on 13 March 2011.

The Times of India (2011), 'Maldives Not in Favour of Chinese Naval Expansion in Indian Ocean', 26 February 2011, available online at http://timesofindia.indiatimes.com/india/Maldives-not-in-favour-of-Chinese-naval-expansion-in-Indian-Ocean/articleshow/7572529.cms, last accessed on 13 December 2011.

Times Online (2011), 'More Lankan Fishermen Freed Today', 5 March 2011, available online at http://sundaytimes.lk/index.php/latest/5280-more-lankan-fishermen-freed-today, last accessed on 6 March 2011.

UNDOALS (United Nations Division for Ocean Affairs and the Law of the Sea) (2007), 'United Nations Convention on the Law of the Sea', available online at www.un.org/Depts/los/convention_agreements/texts/unclos/unclos_e.pdf, last accessed on 11 October 2007.

Vohra, Ravi and V. Srivatsan (eds) (2008), *India–Sri Lanka Maritime Cooperation: Opportunities and Challenges*, Regional Maritime Cooperation Series, New Delhi: National Maritime Foundation.

RCSS PUBLICATIONS

- *Defence, Technology and Cooperative Security in South Asia: Report on the Proceedings of the Tenth Summer Workshop* (RCSS, 2004)
- *Environment Development and Human Security: Perspectives from South Asia* (2003)
- *Terrorism in South Asia: Impact on Development and Democratic Process* (SIPRA, 2003)
- *South Asia and the War on Terrorism* (India Research Press, 2003)
- *Shaping the Future—A South Asian Civil Society Dialogue* (RCSS, July 2002)
- *Small Arms and Human Insecurity* (RCSS, July 2002)
- *SAARC in the Twenty-First Century: Towards a Cooperative Future* (July 2002)
- *Memories of a Genocidal Partition: The Haunting Tale of Victims, Witnesses and Perpetrators* (RCSS, July 2002)
- *South Asian Security Futures: A Dialogue of Director's Regional Strategic Studies Institutes* (March 2002)
- *Globalization and Non-Traditional Security in South Asia* (September 2001)
- *The Simla Agreement. i972: Its Wasted Promise* (Manohar, 2001)
- *Ending the Displacement Cycle: Finding Durable Solutions through Return and Resettlement* (RCSS, 2011)
- *Documents on Sri Lanka's Foreign Policy 1947-1965* (RCSS, 2005)
- *Terrorism in South Asia: Impact on Development and Democratic Process* (RCSS & Konrad Adenauer Foundation, 2003)
- *Environment, Development and Human Security: Perspectives from South Asia* (University Press of America, 2003)

RCSS Policy Studies

50 Extremism in Pakistan and India: The Case of Jamaat-e-Islami and Shiv Sena (RCSS, 2010)
49 Democracy as a Conflict Resolution Model for Terrorism: A Case Study of India and Pakistan (RCSS, 2010)
48 Understanding Suicide Terrorism and Bangladesh and Sri Lanka (RCSS, 2010)
47 India's Security Dilemma vis-à-vis China: A Case of Optimum or Sub-Optimum Restraint? (RCSS, 2009)
46 Beyond the Security Impasse: State, Development and People (RCSS, 2008)
45 Conflict Transformation from Ethnic Movement to Terrorist Movement: Case Studies of Tamils in Sri Lanka and Mohajirs in Pakistan (RCSS, 2008)
44 Indo- US Nuclear Cooperation: Altering Strategic Positioning & Shifting Balance of Power in South Asia (RCSS, 2008)
43 Peace Building in Afghanistan: Revisiting the Global War on Terrorism (RCSS, 2008)
42 Getting to Rapprochement over Kashmir: Is Using the 'China Model' a Viable Alternative? (RCSS, 2007)
41 Role of a Third Party in Conflict Resolution: A Case Study of India and Norway in Sri Lanka (RCSS, 2007)
40 International Non-Governmental Organizations in Arms Control and Disarmament Potential and Viability (RCSS, 2007)
39 India- Pakistan Dialogue: Bringing the Society in (RCSS, 2007)
38 The 'People's War' in Nepal (RCSS, 2006)
37 Impact of Partition Refugees in Pakistan: Struggle for Empowerment and State's Response (Manohar, 2006)
36 Maritime Cooperation between India and Sri Lanka (Manohar, 2006)
35 Nuclear Risk Reduction Measures in South Asia: Problems and Prospects (Manohar,2006)
34 Indo-Pak Conflicts: Ripe to Resolve? (Manohar, 2005)
33 Small Arms and the Security Debate in South Asia (Manohar, 2005)